A CONFUSION OF
PROPHETS

———

A CONFUSION OF PROPHETS

VICTORIAN AND EDWARDIAN ASTROLOGY

PATRICK CURRY

A JULIET GARDINER BOOK

C&B

COLLINS & BROWN

First published in Great Britain in 1992
by Collins & Brown Limited
Mercury House
195 Knightsbridge
London SW7 1RE

This book is printed on partially recycled acid-free paper

A CIP catalogue record for this book
is available from the British Library

ISBN 1 85585 136 9

Typeset by Falcon Graphic Art Limited
Printed and bound in Great Britain by Clays Ltd

CONTENTS

ACKNOWLEDGEMENTS

The following people read either the whole or substantial parts of the book in draft, and it is unquestionably the better for their comments and suggestions: Simon Schaffer, Clay Ramsay, Patricia Fara, Maggie Hyde, Geoffrey Cornelius, Ray Keenoy and Angus Clarke. Other more specific debts will be acknowledged in the course of my references after each chapter.

I am especially grateful to two other readers: my wife, Suzanna, and my editor, Juliet Gardiner. It is thanks to the latter that this book appears in print; to the former, in large part, that I was able to write it.

I would also like to thank the Social Sciences and Humanities Council of Canada for supporting eighteen months of the research this book required.

Finally, my mother Noreen kindly made her flat available as an office while I was writing this book; and my daughter Sylva, who was born the day after I signed the contract, was a delightful distraction throughout.

I would also like to acknowledge the following for their kind permission to reproduce illustrations. Plate 1 appears courtesy of the National Picture Gallery. Plate 3 appears courtesy of the Board of Trustees of the Victoria and Albert Museum. Plate 4 appears courtesy of Lytton Enterprises Ltd. Reproductions and their shelfmarks appearing courtesy of the British Library are as follows: plate 2 (10826.dd.22.), plate 6 (718.g.23.), plate 7 (P.P.2477.y.), plates 8, 9 and 12 (P.P.2477.u.*), plate 11 (8610.ee.21.), plate 15 (P.P.1556.da.) and plate 17 (P.P.1556.dad.).

A cry —
It is new life. With our first breath
We take into ourselves the pain of history.

(John Heath-Stubbs)

Negative capability, that is, when a man is capable of being in uncertainties, mysteries, doubts, without any irritable reaching after fact and reason.

(John Keats)

. . . political victory is equivalent to the elimination of the specifically political nature of the victorious practices.

(Ernesto Laclau)

INTRODUCTION

EARLY IN THE NINETEENTH CENTURY, the visiting American author Washington Irving found that in the heart of London the inhabitants 'still believe in dreams and fortune-telling, and an old woman that lives in Bull-and-Mouth Street makes a tolerable subsistence by detecting stolen goods, and promising the girls good husbands. They are apt to be rendered uncomfortable by comets and eclipses . . . '

Compared to the glory days of astrology 150 years earlier, however, this was a sad decline. Then, a well-known astrologer could expect to number among his clients merchants, members of Parliament and a clutch of gentlemen. By 1815, the only way such people were likely to encounter an astrologer was in Sir Walter Scott's new romantic novel, *Guy Mannering; or, The Astrologer*. Scott's plot hinges partly on the hero's skill in interpreting the stars and it might have had even greater prominence had he not decided, 'on mature consideration, that Astrology, though its influence was once received and admitted by [Francis] Bacon himself, does not now retain influence over the general mind sufficient even to constitute the mainspring of a romance'.

As Guy Mannering himself puts it, in an impeccable historical summary, 'The belief in astrology was almost universal in the middle of the seventeenth century; it began to waver and become doubtful toward the close of that period, and in the beginning of the eighteenth the art fell into general disrepute, and even under general ridicule.' Briefly, what happened was this: for two decades in the mid-seventeenth century, English astrologers achieved undreamt-of influence and respect.

Everywhere, from the street to the court and the House of Commons, the predictions of men like William Lilly (1602–81) were studied and disputed. Like most prominent astrologers of the time, Lilly prophesied for the Roundheads; a few favoured the king, while others belonged to the radical sects.

With the Restoration of Charles II in 1660, however, astrology began a long and disastrous fall from favour. The Church took advantage of more settled times to reaffirm its customary opposition; after some dithering, the natural philosophers of the Royal Society also returned a negative verdict. But most important, in the minds of the upper and middle classes, astrologers had come to be associated with the chaos and sedition of the Civil War period. As the marriage between those two classes became cemented by the Glorious Revolution of 1688–9 and the long reign of the Georges, astrology as a species of what was called 'enthusiasm' became inexorably considered more 'vulgar'. By the mid-eighteenth century, it was confined almost entirely to the semi-literate labouring class, in the form of popular beliefs concerning the phases of the Moon and other readily visible phenomena.

This world-view was found mainly among the rural population, although there were urban believers too. The people Washington Irving mentions continued to swear by *Old Moore's Almanack* or *Vox Stellarum*, a successor, in several varieties, to the original almanac begun by Francis Moore in 1699. It sold hundreds of thousands of copies every year throughout the nineteenth century.

But this was not the only kind of astrology; and it is not the subject of this book. A more complex and sophisticated set of rules for interpreting the positions of the planets — usually at birth, in what were called 'nativities' — constitutes what is properly called judicial astrology, because it involves the astrologer having to make a judgement. Originally Babylonian, it was revised and systematized by the later Greeks, especially Ptolemy, refined by a number of medieval Arabic and Renaissance European authorities, and again by the great astrologers of the seventeenth century: Lilly and John Partridge in England, Jean-Baptiste Morin in France and others. As Scott remarked, a more central place for this subject in his novel would indeed have 'involved doctrines and discussions of a nature too serious for [my] purpose, and for the character of the narrative'.

He added, as 'worthy of observation, that while the astrological doctrines have fallen into general contempt, and been supplanted by superstitions of a more gross and far less beautiful character, they have, even in modern days, retained some votaries'. In this, too, he was correct. Judicial astrology survived the eighteenth century in provincial pockets of Leicestershire and Lincolnshire, and among a few isolated *aficionados* in London. At the end of the century, there were again a few books in print on the subject by two professional judicial astrologers: Ebenezer Sibly (1751–99) and John Worsdale (1766–c.1828). Their readership was tiny but loyal.

What Scott did not anticipate, however, was the remarkable rebirth of judicial astrology in England's towns and cities. Beginning in the 1830s, judicial astrologers with exotic *noms de plume* like Raphael, Zadkiel and Alan Leo struggled to create a new niche for the ancient art. They demonstrably failed to convince the opinion-makers and enforcers of the day, but in other respects their success was impressive: their consultancies were busy, their textbooks reprinted, and their annual almanacs sold tens of thousands of copies every year. Although astrology was scorned by one late-nineteenth-century newspaper as merely 'a crazy old lady, still jogging along the highway of life', there was clearly a dance in the old dame yet. By now, in the words of another newspaper in 1910, there was in London 'a confusion of prophets'. This renaissance was overwhelmingly a metropolitan phenomenon, which is why I have been able to concentrate on London without distorting the overall picture or omitting anything important.

This book closes in the early decades of the twentieth century. By then astrology, in much the same form and despite official disapproval and even persecution, was the universal and tolerated fixture it is today. In fact, as a going concern it has outlasted many of its occult contemporaries. For Victorian and Edwardian England also saw a boom in mediumship, phrenology and spiritualism, as well as the founding of the Society for Psychical Research and the Theosophical Society. Magic and the supernatural also appeared in the most popular novels of the day. To many of its adherents, of course, astrology was only one part of this heady mix. But it had a life of its own too, with its own ideas, practitioners and clients. That is what I focus on, referring to other occult pursuits only when they overlap with the study of the stars.

Both the astrologers and their clients came, broadly speaking, from the urban middle classes. Although a few astrologers moved in quite distinguished circles, most did not. The Reverend Charles Davies described one he visited in 1875, living in 'a cosy house' in Newington Causeway:

> Clad in a light overcoat, with spectacles on his nose, and bending over his MS., Professor Smith [a pseudonym] might have been a dissenting parson en deshabillé 'getting off' his Sunday discourse, or a village schoolmaster correcting the 'themes' of his pupils ... As he rose to receive us I was almost disappointed to find that he held no wand, wore no robe, and had no volume of mystic lore by his side. The very cat that emerged from underneath his table, and rubbed itself against my legs was not of the orthodox sable, but simple tabby and white.

Although otherwise unexceptional, such a social background for the reappearance of astrology is striking, given the overwhelmingly rural and uneducated character of astrology's previous constituency. I describe this phenomenon as the appearance of a new type: the middle-class occultist. In the words of one of the new publications capitalizing on this market, *Old Moore's Monthly Messenger*,

> it has been brought to my notice that in the higher circles of Society (unless I am borrowed from the kitchen or surreptitiously taken out of the pocket for private perusal) I am, in my humble garb of a penny or twopenny almanack, seldom permitted to shine forth (as I am told I ought to) in the upper parts of the mansion. This has determined me to put on once a month a fashionable coat; not exactly

a court suit but garments that will shew due respect to my new clientele.

The same social backdrop also highlights the peculiarity of the persecution which nineteenth-century astrologers frequently faced, when they were entrapped by police officers posing as clients. The usual sentence was up to three months' hard labour, with no appeal allowed. Given astrologers' otherwise innocuous character and behaviour, their offence can only be described as a kind of thought-crime, namely 'believing in astrology'. It was the sort of situation that these days might attract the attention of human rights organizations.

When astrology fell from grace in the late seventeenth and eighteenth centuries, the words most often used to describe it were 'superstition', 'enthusiasm' and 'ignorance'. Such words reflected its stigmatization by the religious, political and scientific authorities respectively. In the nineteenth century, this process acquired a new legal dimension. Coincident with the rise of its new urban incarnation, astrology became criminalized through the use of an obscure part of a Georgian Act 'for the Punishment of idle and Disorderly Persons, and Rogues and Vagabonds . . . ' Section 4 of the Vagrancy Act of 1824 (5 G.IV, c.83) specifies that the statute applies to 'every Person pretending or professing to tell Fortunes, or using any subtle Craft, Means, or Device, by Palmistry or otherwise, to deceive and impose on any of His Majesty's Subjects . . . ' From the middle of the nineteenth century until the early twentieth, astrologers stood in real danger of prosecution and imprisonment. The Act had been intended to deal with homeless vagrants and gypsies, whereas the astrologers were usually otherwise respectable householders with the right to vote. However, this was no defence; and their attempts to amend or repeal the relevant section repeatedly failed.

Note too the wording of the Act, which states that one can only 'pretend or profess' to tell fortunes; it is therefore not something that can be done legitimately, or properly speaking at all. Thus the *Daily Telegraph* of 16 July 1875, mentioning a sale of works by John Varley's younger brother Cornelius, remarked typically that 'The elder, indeed, pretended to skill in "judicial astrology", and was consulted by many believers in that art.'

The principal reason for this uncompromising stance lay in the increasing power of the professional middle classes in Victorian England, with their stress on respectability, prudence, industry and progress. As the guardians of the morals and intellect of the country, their duty was to curb and if possible redeem both the undeserving rich and the undeserving poor. An important element in imperialism's crusade on behalf of 'civilization' as against 'barbarism', this attitude was as far-reaching at home as it was abroad. Discussing the persistence of English superstition, for example, the *Athenaeum* of 14 June 1879 noted: 'The ridicule that is heaped on astrology is to be regarded rather as an attraction than a deterrent, for ridicule has never kept back *the high vulgar, or the low*, from believing anything that is absurd.' It was the very fact that the new astrologers were themselves middle class (and, as such, should know better) that was intolerable and required strong measures. It was only with the 'decadence' of the Edwardians that some relaxation became apparent.

Not coincidentally, women astrologers begin to assume equal importance with men at about the same time. It is a startling measure of male dominance in nineteenth-century England that it extended even to the underworld, so to speak, of occultism. It was Madame Blavatsky, and after her Annie Besant, who finally broke that mould. But astrology, as a relatively intellectual divinatory art with some scientific aspirations, was more susceptible to this dominance than some others, such as spiritualism, in which a woman's supposedly intuitive and irrational nature gave her an edge.

Section 4 of the Vagrancy Act quietly disappeared as part of the Statute Law (Repeals) Bill on 16 November 1989, after the Law Commission's working party reported 'widespread agreement' that it should be repealed without replacement. Astrologers did not even notice it had gone until early in 1991, which is a measure of how things have changed. Perhaps they should be more appreciative. As recently as 7 June 1991, but in words that ring down through the centuries, the *Daily Express* snarled that 'Astrologers, and the rest of the fortune-telling caboodle, are free to frighten us into staying at home with our heads under the covers. The Home Secretary must act now and muzzle these pests. Confine them to their kennels.' (This appeared a few pages away from the daily sun-sign column.)

Even when not faced with prosecution, astrologers in the nineteenth century found themselves in a hostile climate of mainstream educated and élite opinion. Some of the questions which I explore, then, are: what did belief in astrology (however qualified) offer its adherents that they evidently did not find in more orthodox places? More broadly, how does the existence of astrology help us better to understand nineteenth-century English society and culture? And, more precisely, how did the divinatory or symbolic aspects of astrological practice adapt to the dominant materialism and scientism, on the one hand, and to religious orthodoxy on the other? (By scientism I mean not the practice but the cult of science, which lays sole claim to the truth.)

Guy Mannering's solution to the last problem was one such attempt, and delightfully ambiguous. He had been taught astrology while young by an old clergyman-astrologer, and became skilled (a possibility the Vagrancy Act attempted to foreclose) 'before he became convinced of its absurdity'. Seeing the danger foretold in the nativity of his host, the laird's son, Mannering therefore 'resolved plainly to tell him the judgement which he had formed, while at the same time acquainting him with the futility of the rules of the art on which he had proceeded'.

My primary purpose, however, is simpler. It is to present and explore the world of the astrologers themselves, their followers, patrons and critics. These people constituted a fascinating mental and cultural underworld in nineteenth-century England, especially in London. So why is it that these particular Victorians and Edwardians have remained almost invisible?

There are a couple of reasons. First, because the categories usually used by social historians are inadequate — too much of people's inner life is simply left out. And second, because of an attitude, usually described as 'anachronism', that encourages intellectuals to ignore, or even simply not notice, aspects of the past which they dislike or do not understand in the present. Our contemporary reluctance to take 'superstition' seriously is not very different from its Victorian counterpart; in fact, it owes much to the latter. If every age gets the past it deserves, by now we deserve better.

True, my astrologers and their clientele were of no great global consequence; they were not leading players on the world stage. But I agree with Barrington Moore, Jr, that 'For all students of human society, sympathy with the victims of historical processes and scepticism about the victors' claims provide essential safeguards against being taken in by the dominant mythology.' Since the society I study here was dominated by a mythology largely shared between religion and science, it is those claims which most need a dose of doubt. (If astrology ever replaced them as the dominant mythology and scientists were obliged as a result to ply their trade in furtive and precarious ways, the latter would deserve correspondingly more sympathy and the former more scepticism.)

It is not often recognized how much modern science, with its attempted monopoly of the truth, has borrowed from the one God of Judaeo-Christianity. As an unrepentant pluralist and relativist, however, it seems to me that a world dominated by a single vision of any kind, with no room for the apparently eccentric or insignificant — whether now or in the past — is not a world worth living in. For that reason too, such people as astrologers are not only worthy of sympathetic consideration, but may be those who need it most.

As for the question which sometimes arises in connection with this kind of subject — namely, Do you believe in it? — I would be foolish to accept its terms by answering either yes or no. At best, the question is *mal posée*; 'belief' is at once too broad and too weak a term. At worst, and more usually, it is a crude attempt to identify you with one side or the other of a fruitless and boring game, played between self-styled defenders of science-and-reason on the one hand and of esoteric spirituality on the other. Concerning the people in this book, therefore, my reply would be that I believe passionately in their right to believe as they did. In short, I believe in their belief.

I have therefore aimed at depth without esotericism, rigour without scientism, and a faithful account of the conundrums of human experience above all.

CHAPTER I

JOHN VARLEY: MAGUS

IT IS THE MORNING OF 21 June 1825. In his studio — one of the several rooms he has leased in Great Titchfield Street, in London's West End — the artist John Varley is going over his calculations for the day yet again. At eleven o'clock he calls for his son Albert. Varley gives him his pocket-watch, telling him to take it to a watchmaker's in nearby Regent Street and have it set precisely by Greenwich time. When the young man returns, his father is still pacing up and down the room.

Finally Varley remarks, 'I can't make it out.' He explains to his bewildered son that there is an evil aspect in his horoscope that day, which comes into operation at a few minutes to noon. The problem is that the planet menacing him is Uranus which, having only recently been discovered, he says, is not yet properly understood by astrologers. His reading of the aspect has revealed only that the danger will be sudden and serious. Therefore he has already decided to forgo his morning's appointment and stay indoors. 'But whether the danger is to me personally or to my property,' he concludes, 'I cannot tell.'

Twelve o'clock approaches. Varley becomes still more restless and his son more worried. At a few minutes before noon, he sits down and says, 'I feel quite well, there's nothing the matter with me. Could I have made a mistake?' and reaches for his papers and a pencil. At that moment, there is a cry of 'Fire!' from outside. They run out into the street, only to discover that it is their own house that is in flames from a fire at the piano factory next door. Varley's response is delight and satisfaction, and to his son's consternation he immediately returns to his desk to write a quick account of his discovery. By the time it is all over, Varley has lost his home and all of his property, none of which was insured. More importantly, however — in his view — he has verified both the precision of his methods of timing and the evil potentialities of the new planet. Meeting Varley later, the painter Copley Fielding asked if the loss was serious. 'No,' he replied, 'only the house burned down. I knew something would happen.'

John Varley is usually remembered today as a skilled and influential artist. A founder member of the Society of Painters in Water-Colours, his drawings and paintings of romantic rural landscapes still have a respected place in British art history. Varley the astrologer, however, has all but disappeared. Yet that role was at least as important in his eyes, and in those of his contemporaries. With a mixture of curiosity, fear and derision, his prophetic skills were sometimes sought, sometimes avoided, but in either case they were an accepted fixture in London's social scene during the early decades of the nineteenth century.

Varley was born at 3.34 p.m. on 17 August 1778, in a former inn called The Blue Posts in Hackney, then a suburban village of London. Through his mother, he was a descendant of the General Fleetwood who married Oliver Cromwell's daughter Bridget. The family was proud of its kinship with Cromwell and continued to maintain a sturdy independence of mind and politics. Varley's father Richard was tutor to the radical and republican third Earl Stanhope; later, his son taught both art and astrology to the earl's favourite child, Lady Hester Stanhope.

Varley's life as a boy was remarkable only for the early appearance of talent in two respects: draughtsmanship and boxing. The latter was accompanied — fortunately, given his size and strength — by a characteristic commitment to peace and fair play, if necessary by force. His efforts on behalf of the bullied soon earned him the respect of his peers. Probably, it also stood his younger brothers in good stead: Cornelius, later a successful watchmaker, optician and scientist, who invented the Graphic Telescope, a two-prism device for drawing objects precisely; and William, also a water-colourist. In addition, there were two sisters, of whom the elder, Elizabeth, was herself an artist.

In 1791, after the death of Varley's father Richard, the family moved to Old Street in East London. Nine years later, John and Cornelius decamped, first to Charles Street, Covent Garden, then, the following year, to 2 Harris Place, just off Oxford Street. In 1803, Varley married Esther Gisbourne. She came from a musical and literary family. Her two sisters married the painter Copley Fielding and the composer Clementi; and, through their brother John, Varley soon met the Shelleys and Godwins. He and Esther had five sons and three daughters; the eldest, Albert Fleetwood Varley (1804–76), became one of his father's chief witnesses and recorders. Living frugally, the Varleys occupied a succession of places in central London: from 1805 until about 1814, in Broad Street, near Golden Square in Soho; then Conduit Street; and in 1817, Great Titchfield Street. Esther died in July 1824 and the following year Varley married again, this time a neighbour, the daughter of the engraver Wilson Lowry. In 1831, forced out by a second fire, they moved to 3 Elkins Road in Bayswater.

Varley had grown up into a big man — about seventeen stone in weight — with a heart to match. One observer, perhaps somewhat unkindly, suggested that his physique when stooping over some work suggested the rear view of an elephant. Later, another wrote that as an older man Varley had a face like shattered rock, with wistful eyes. Incongruously, he spoke with a pronounced childish lisp and, making no concessions to dress-etiquette or fashion, he went everywhere in a huge great-coat, its pockets stuffed with almanacs. Yet he seems to have been widely welcomed. Despite his complete lack of interest in Christian faith or doctrine, it was universally agreed that Varley was unfailingly generous, broad-minded and kind.

These qualities attracted a swarm of borrowers with hard-luck stories. Allied to an extremely poor sense of economy, they caused him life-long problems with creditors; to avoid them Varley was sometimes obliged to lead a preposterous life of stealth. He once remarked to his friend and fellow-artist John Linnell, 'Well, thank God, I am nearly out of debt. I have only two writs against me, and one judgement upon which my goods can be seized; and the lawyer is such a good fellow that he will wait if I give him a picture . . . ' He also invented a novel but characteristic method of obtaining payment from wealthy but 'forgetful' debtors: 'I send in a new bill,' he explained, 'making a mistake in the amount of a guinea or two *against myself*, and the money comes in directly.'

Varley's income came from the sale of his pictures and his tuition fees. The younger students shared his home. If Varley had a religion, it was pantheism, and he urged his pupils to draw 'everything in nature, and in every mood'. The better-known included Linnell, William Mulready, who married Varley's sister Elizabeth, William Henry Hunt, and, briefly, Samuel Palmer, whose wife Hannah was Linnell's eldest daughter. Mulready became particularly close; they engaged in boxing as well as artistic bouts, and Mulready once saved his friend from drowning when he had a cramp while swimming in the Thames.

Varley's enthusiasm for landscape painting was infectious, sometimes inspiring the servants as well as the masters or mistresses to try their hand. To those boarding students, however, he was a hard taskmaster who laid about him indiscriminately (or perhaps democratically) in response to any undue noise or disorder while working. On at least one occasion, even the dog fell foul of him, Varley remarking, 'I *hate* affectation.' He worked long and hard hours; his production of paintings for the annual shows of the Society of Painters in Water-Colours was prodigious. Sometimes, a friend recalled,

> that he might get on with his work, his dinner was sent into his study. There lay together in a pleasant confusion 'curious books', deep twilights, and fruit pie: a bit snatched now and then in the intervals of very solemn talk about tolling Curlews, setting Moons, or MacBeth's castle in its inspissated gloom.

Occasionally, Varley would visit a stately home to teach drawing to its wealthy proprietors. One such was Cranford House in Middlesex, where the elder branch of the Berkeley family resided. Grantley Berkeley recalled that one day,

When walking with Mr Hughes, he encountered my hounds running a red deer. He had not the least idea that men on horseback rode over fences, and was speechless with admiration at the collected way in which Brutus leaped a flight of rails by the inn, and then the hedge and ditch into the road where he was standing. The cry of the hounds, the cheer of the huntsman, which I gave rather to astonish him than to excite the hounds, who were running hard, and the notes of the horn, roused him up and drove him wild with excitement; and I presently beheld him running in the wake of the hounds like a boy. He called the members of the hunt 'the personifications of the Centaur'.

If Nature was his god, and art his homage and livelihood, astrology for John Varley was a passion and a way of life. There is no evidence that he ever took any money for it, and every probability that he did not. Every morning, upon arising, he would sit and work out his directions and transits for the day. In the words of his art-dealer and close friend William Vokins,

Distinguished people frequenting my house of business would beg to be introduced to him, not more for his artistic celebrity than for his astrological knowledge, and for the interest there was in the man himself, for he was a most genial spirit. Astrology was a mania with him, and his common theme at table. He was no sooner introduced to a stranger than he asked him the date of his birth, and having obtained that knowledge, he soon made out the stranger's horoscope.

His contemporary James Ward confirms that 'Varley was rarely introduced to anyone that he did not in a short time ask them for the day and hour of their birth.'

John Constable, the eminent painter, wrote in a letter on 22 August, 1831 that

I have bought a little drawing of John Varley — the conjurer — who is now a beggar — but a fat and sturdy one — He told me how to do landscape and was so kind as to point out all my defects — The price of a little drawing was a Guinea and a half, but a Guinea only to an Artist — however I insisted on his taking the larger sum, as he had clearly proved to me that I was no artist!!

Obviously a man who gives unsolicited advice at some length to Constable on improving his technique is not easily abashed. In a letter of 5 October 1822, Elizabeth Turner, later Lady Palgrave, wrote:

> With all his nobility of mind he unites a more than childish simplicity, and he entirely believes in astrology, palmistry, the raising of ghosts and seeing of visions . . . and this part of his character lies open at first sight, for he dashes at once into astrology, and was not happy until he had cast all our nativities, yet he is quite sane in mind even on this insane topic . . .

As Constable's epithet of 'conjurer' implies, Varley was probably better known during his life as an astrologer than as an artist; although it is difficult to say, for his professional connections among the nobility were inseparable from his astrological. As Varley himself admitted, 'Ladies come to take drawing lessons that they may get their nativities cast!' Similarly, his students referred to him as 'Vates' — prophet or seer — and many of those calling to view his pictures were in reality drawn by his astrological fame. Even among sceptics, Varley never lost an opportunity to test his powers, increase his knowledge or convert the reluctant. He would draw up the person's nativity in a matter of ten minutes or so — he always carried the necessary books with him — and, after studying it, he would pronounce either predictions concerning his or her future or, in some cases, comments on the hidden past. Sometimes he would first infer the person's time of birth from their appearance, or even correct them as to their true time of birth, on the same basis.

This procedure was based on the ancient idea that one's physical appearance, among other attributes, is closely related to the 'ascendant', or the sign of the zodiac that was rising on the eastern horizon at the time of birth, which in turn is determined by the time, not the date, of birth. As Varley writes:

> It is erroneously imagined that peoples can be born under that sign only

> in which the Sun is located at the time of their birth; whereas they are astrologically and correctly said to be born under that sign and degree of the Zodiac, which was rising in the east at their birth . . . Therefore, as all the signs rise and set once in every twenty-four hours, a person may be born under any sign, on any day in the year.

The signs of the Zodiac fall into four groups, associated with the four elements and humours: fire (choleric), earth (phlegmatic), air (sanguine) and water (melancholic). This in turn gives rise to four basic temperaments and types for humankind at large. In Varley's descriptions, these are fiery ('spirited, generous, magnanimous, princely'), earthy ('careful, sordid, penurious'), airy ('humane, harmonious, courteous') and watery ('cold, prolific, cautious, severe'). He adds sadly that the earthy and watery types are encountered more frequently.

Varley made a special investigation of this subject, which he believed should properly be termed a branch of natural philosophy. The first part of his study — four were planned — appeared in 1828, entitled *A Treatise on Zodiacal Physiognomy, illustrated with engravings of heads and features, accompanied by tables of the time of the rising of the Twelve Signs of the Zodiac; and containing also new and astrological explanations of some remarkable portions of ancient mythological history*. It included tables for determining one's rising sign without calculations, 'to enable the public to judge, equally with the astrologians, of the zodiacal classification of the human race'.

This book was recently described as one of the most widely ignored ever written and its lack of success may have discouraged Varley from publishing its sequel. To quote the synopsis, it was to have contained 'A list of a Portion of the Classic Fables and Sacred Histories of which an entirely new and Detailed explanation is prepared for publication, from Discoveries founded on the Application of Astrological Knowledge, and on the ancient Theban art of Geomancy, by John Varley.' (Geomancy is usually divination by means of dots and lines on paper. Originally, it involved throwing earth on a surface and interpreting the resulting patterns.) This manuscript apparently existed as late as 1910 and it may well have influenced W.B. Yeats's magico-historical theories. It is tantalizing to note that one of Varley's sons, John Varley Jr, married Yeats's maternal aunt, Isabella Pollexfen.

The illustrations in the *Treatise* include an engraving by John Linnell which was based on the bizarre portrait of the 'Ghost of a Flea' by William Blake. Varley comments that Gemini is its significator. As he later told a friend,

> I called on him one evening, and found Blake more than usually excited. He told me that he had seen a wonderful thing — the ghost of a flea! And did you make a drawing of him? I enquired. No, indeed, said he, I wish I had, but I shall, if he appears again! He looked earnestly into a corner of the room, and then said, here he is — reach me my things — I shall keep my eye on him. There he comes! his eager tongue whisking out of his mouth, a cup in his hand to hold blood, and covered with a scaly skin of gold and green; — as he described him, so he drew him.

In 1818, William Blake was living in South Molton Street, very near Varley in Great Titchfield Street. (Blake had been born nearby at 28 Broad Street, off Golden Square.) Linnell introduced the two men that year, and despite their decided differences in temperament, outlook and age — Varley was twenty years younger — they became close friends and remained so until Blake's death in 1827. It was in Varley's studio that their collaboration on the so-called 'Visionary Heads' took place.

Blake and Varley make a fascinating study of contrasts. They were equally concerned with the spiritual world, or the spiritual aspect of this world, but approached it very differently. Where Varley's natural inclination was naturalistic and objective, tending perhaps to literal-minded, that of Blake was visionary, with the imagination taking at least equal status to that of mundane reality. The result was hours of argument — as shown in the sketch by Linnell — which both doubtless thoroughly enjoyed. Typically, while Blake conceded the reality of astral influence, he disputed what he considered to be Varley's materialistic understanding of it. 'Your fortunate nativity', Blake declared. 'I count the worst. You reckon that to be born in August' — i.e. under the royal sign of

Leo — 'and have the notice and patronage of kings to be the best of all; whereas the lives of the Apostles and martyrs, of whom it is said the world was not worthy, would be counted by you as the worst, and their nativities those of men born to be hanged.' However, the converse also held true: neither Blake nor Linnell could make any dent in Varley's profound lack of interest in Christianity. Astrology's ancient affiliation to pagan polytheism, with the planets seen as gods, is not coincidental here. To such an outlook, Judaeo-Christian monotheism is unattractive at best and tyrannical at worst.

If Varley had been a less generous man, he might have envied Blake's more immediate and direct access to those immaterial realities which he was obliged merely to infer. But Varley could still desire to render them more tangible to his own and others' 'mortal and perishing eye', in Blake's disparaging term. As he wrote in *Zodiacal Physiognomy*, 'I was anxious to make the most correct investigation in my power, of the truth of these visions . . . ' And he had another powerful incentive: Blake's visionary faculty provided a unique opportunity for research into the zodiacal physiognomy of long-lost remarkable personages — heroes, villains, beauties — whose features, revealing their strength of character, would offer striking zodiacal insights. Blake too was interested in this subject; he had already read a standard work on physiognomy and bought Spurzheim's new book on phrenology a year earlier.

Varley therefore hit upon a plan. Having settled Blake in his own studio, usually between nine or ten at night and early the next morning, and provided him with pencil and paper, he would ask him, for instance, to draw Moses. If the spirits were co-operating, Blake would respond, 'There he is!' and begin drawing rapidly in sure strokes, exactly as if the person was sitting before him. Varley, for his part, would try to note the moment that the vision appeared. From that time, he would later calculate the degree of the zodiac rising at that moment, providing a kind of metaphorical ascendant, which could then be compared with the visage in question. It was not always possible to pursue this course; sometimes the spirits came thick and fast, often unbidden, and disputed the right to be drawn. While drawing William Wallace, for example,

Blake suddenly stopped and said, 'I cannot finish him — Edward the First has stepped in between him and me.' Thinking quickly, Varley replied, 'That's lucky, for I want the portrait of Edward too.' So, with a fresh sheet of paper, Blake obliged; whereupon His Majesty vanished and Blake resumed his portrait of Wallace.

Despite such unforeseen, not to say irregular interruptions, Blake and Varley's collaborative spiritual research — only incidentally artistic to the participants — was carried out in a systematic way, mostly between October 1819 and August 1820. The result was an extraordinary set of portraits, many of which were only rediscovered in 1989. As described by Varley in his scribbled notes, the timed portraits include 'Wat Tyler by Blake, from his spectre, as in the act of striking the tax gatherer, drawn October 30, 1819, 1 a.m.'; 'The Man Who Built the Pyramids, Oct. 18, 1819. fiteeen degrees of Cancer ascending'; 'the Empress Maud . . . Octr. 29 Friday. 11 pm. 1819'; 'Cassibelane the British Chief, By Blake, Octr. 27. 1819/11 p.m.'; and 'Richard Coeur de Lion, drawn from his spectre — W. Blake fecit, Oct. 14, 1819, at a quarter past twelve, midnight.'

There are no surviving astrological maps for these; the only map we have by Varley's own hand is his nativity of Hannah Palmer, given to her father John Linnell in 1838. I therefore took the liberty of having some drawn up, as Varley must have done. The one for Richard the Lion-Heart proved very interesting. The non-astrologer should appreciate a couple of points here. Firstly, it is widely accepted that the most personal, if not necessarily the most significant points in a map are those which change the fastest, namely the ascendant and its corollary the mid-heaven (which change signs every two hours) and then the Moon (which does so about every two-and-a-half days). Secondly, Richard's sobriquet is the only name of those portrayed to contain a direct reference to astrological symbolism: Leo, the lion. This map — for 12.15 a.m., 14 October 1819, Soho — has Leo both ascending and containing the Moon.

Of course, it may be that Varley, knowing the astrological circumstances, deliberately asked Blake for Richard's portrait at that time. But it is also possible that the king simply made his appearance then.

Unfortunately, it is not possible for us to know which was the case. If the latter, Varley would certainly have seen the result as confirming the correctness of both traditional astrological symbolism and his own particular practice, although in equating the time of the spirit's appearance with that of its 'birth', Varley was making a move perhaps more in keeping with the spirit than the letter of astrology.

Zodiacal physiognomy was only one of Varley's astrological concerns. The chief one was judicial astrology, which involves making judgements, whether as to the past, present or future, from a map of the sky at a particular moment — often, though not necessarily, that of birth. And there can be little doubt that John Varley was a master of this art. Based not only on his record, but also on the grasp of traditional astrology that his *Treatise* reveals, he ranks with the most eminent (or notorious) of his predecessors in the seventeenth century, such as William Lilly.

Within his own lifetime, profound social and cultural changes had already reduced Lilly from an object of fear and respect to a figure of fun. Varley lived and practised entirely within such constraints. He was well aware of them: 'It is a rare circumstance,' he wrote, 'to find anyone among the numerous enemies of astrology, who, when asked, is not compelled to acknowledge that he is entirely ignorant of the principles of the science which he has the temerity and confidence to condemn.' It is therefore not just a difference of accident and temperament between the two men that has left us with a considerable body of Lilly's own much earlier writings but almost none by Varley. The historical circumstances that rendered him little more than a harmless and eccentric buffoon continue to operate today. As a master of something which had been declared impossible, and therefore non-existent, Varley's true stature was difficult even to perceive, let alone admit. To the extent that we have now moved on, we may do better.

Ironically, Varley's own approach to the study of astrology, and his understanding of what he was doing, was in many respects 'scientific', i.e. systematic, empirical, and so on. A working scientist recently wrote:

any scientist who understands his work must be fundamentally religious, although not necessarily in the sense of classical religion. Science uncovers the work and art of a grand designer, exposing a reality of such sheer beauty and economy that it drives many scientists to become totally immersed in their work.

One may doubt whether many scientists understand their work in quite this fashion, but as an idea, in nearly every respect — Nature as divine, her beauty and economy, the worker's total immersion — this passage describes Varley perfectly. The only exception is the existence of a single grand designer, which he would probably have declined to infer. Of course, philosophers and apologists of science have laid waste whole forests trying to distinguish between 'real' science and 'pseudoscience' on the basis of supposedly irreconcilable differences in their proponents' methods. The fact is, however, that Varley was deemed superstitious and credulous not because of his methodology but because of his identity, subject-matter and conclusions. These being astrological, they were, by that token, unacceptable.

But what was Varley really doing, in so far as we can tell, as an astrologer? What was his practice? Let us consider some instances. The following stories have been confirmed either by their subjects or by more than one person, usually witnesses and always contemporaries. Of course, we do not know how many of his astrological predictions failed to come true. On the other hand, even if by some miracle we did, the resulting statistical calculation would tell us only how likely or unlikely was their fulfilment — not whether or not they did, nor how they were arrived at, nor their effects.

One morning, before setting out on a walk and after his habit of checking his own nativity for the day, Varley remarked to two friends: 'We shall witness some horrible accident before we get back.' Later that day, as they broke off their walk to watch some work on a railway bridge, a workman, leaning over one of the piles, was crushed by a piledriver hammer which had been accidently released.

On another occasion, the astrologer was present in the house of his friend William Vokins when his daughter was born and immediately cast the child's nativity. After studying it, he turned to her father and said, 'Be very careful of the child when she is four years of age. At that time she will be in danger of a severe accident from fire.' Not surprisingly, perhaps, the parents ignored or had forgotten Varley's injunction when, during the year mentioned, the little girl was severely scalded. She lost both sight and hearing, before eventually recovering the use of her eyes.

Predictions could be trivial as well as momentous. Calling one day on a picture-dealer, whether Vokins or not is not known, Varley tried to sell him some drawings he had brought in a portfolio. Despite repeated urgings, the dealer declined to purchase; whereupon the artist exclaimed, 'I shall sell before I leave the house!' mentioning that a current aspect from a transmitting planet warranted it. The dealer, fascinated but still refusing to buy, offered Varley tea; then, just as he was finally about to leave, a friend of the dealer's dropped in. Upon being introduced, he immediately bought the artist's pictures. 'Ah!' exclaimed Varley triumphantly, 'I told you I should sell before I left your house.'

More than one story concerns his son Albert, who is, through his own son John (1850–1933), their source. On one occasion, when Albert was a boy, Varley sent him to deliver two important drawings to the gentleman who had commissioned them. Upon arriving, he found that the drawings had slipped out of the portfolio and were lost. Returning slowly home, he steeled himself to tell his father, who was a strict disciplinarian to his children as well as himself. When he appeared, Varley asked, 'Did you deliver the drawings?' To the boy's relief, however, the artist quietly interrupted his stammerings: 'No, you did not deliver them. I was looking at my figure for the day, after you left, and I saw that you should lose them. I shall never see them again. But it was not your fault, but mine.'

Such an incident naturally made a considerable impression on Varley's son — an impression that was further strengthened many years later, when Albert was a bachelor living in rooms. He had a bad cold and, catching a chemist just before he shut up shop, Albert took the medicine away without waiting for the doctor's instructions. Arriving home, he took the entire remedy and went to bed. He awoke the next day feeling wretched and was startled to find his father — who rarely ventured out of his studio in daylight hours — shaking him. 'I was looking over your horoscope,' he said, 'and found directions pointing to your death or very great danger today, so I came to see what had happened!' Upon hearing Albert's story, Varley immediately sent for food, stimulants and a doctor, who credited his father's intervention with saving Albert's health if not his life.

At other times, Varley's astrological acuteness received testimony, albeit not always positive, from other recipients. Edward Scriven, a notable engraver, declared that facts about his personal life which could only have been known by himself were none the less confided to him by Varley, in some detail, on the basis of his nativity. So many of Varley's predictions concerning his children came true that James Ward, the animal-painter, destroyed the horoscopes. Like many religious men in preceding centuries, he decided that Varley's success was evidence of an unholy collusion with the Devil.

There was undeniably an element of fatalism in many of Varley's forecasts. His country host, Grantley Berkeley, recounted:

> one man, to avoid a prediction of his, that an accident was to happen at a particular time, lay in bed all day; but in the evening, thinking that the dangerous hour had gone by, having risen to go downstairs, he tumbled over his own coal-scuttle, and rolling to the first landing-place, strained his ankle very severely — fulfilling the prophecy to the letter.

In a later and otherwise unsubstantiated version, this happened to Varley himself.

Strangely, Varley's accuracy apparently slipped when dealing with astrology itself. After his expulsion from Oxford in 1841, Sir Richard Burton, the explorer and orientalist, went to see 'old Mr Varley, the artist, of whom I was very fond'. He recalled that on one occasion, 'Mr Varley drew out my horoscope and prognosticated that I was to become a great astrologer; but the prophecy came to nothing, for although I had read Cornelius Agrippa and others of the same school at Oxford, I found Zadkiel quite sufficient for me.'

John Ruskin was more impressed. He wrote that, aged about twenty-three,

> chancing to call with Dr Acland on John Varley, the conversation falling on his favourite science of astrology, and we both laughing at it, he challenged either of us to give him the place and hour of our nativity, saying that, if either could, he could prove the truth of the science in ten minutes. I happened to be able to give mine, and in certainly not more than ten minutes, occupied in drawing the diagram of its sky, he fastened upon the three years of my past life when I was fourteen, eighteen, and twenty-one, as having been especially fatal to me.
>
> These were the years in which I first saw in Paris, secondly in London, staying with us in our Herne Hill house, and, thirdly, lost by her marriage, the French girl to whom certain very foolish love-poems were written, which my least wise friends plague me now to reprint. But the three periods of crisis were only foci in the general mistake, mismanagement and misfortune of all my education, precisely between those years from the age of fourteen to twenty-one . . . The girl being once fairly married, and which was of more importance — I beginning to feel a little how foolish and wicked I had been, I took myself up in returning from Italy over the Cenis in 1841, and finding breath and spirit suddenly stronger in a scorching morning at Lans-le-bourg, I date from that hour and place the beginning of my vital work and education.

Is it irrelevant that Ruskin, who described himself as 'a Tory of the old school', brought up on Scott and Homer, permitted himself to be impressed? More readily, at any rate, than the 'modern' and liberal acolytes of progress whom we shall meet later. But Ruskin had other reasons too. He was already convinced of the spiritual vitality of Greek myths, which he contrasted with the poverty of modern scientific materialism. Whereas the lives of the Greeks were directed by the Sun, he felt, we have only the 'guttered candle-ends of Bishops' and the gaslight of Parliament, it being 'the final act and outcome of lowest national atheism, since it cannot deny the Sun, at least to strive to do without it'. And in 1867, Ruskin wrote to Henry Acland: 'If the nation can heartily believe that even the Sun is God (like poor Turner) and act on such belief — and make Sun-Bishops, with eyes — it may see its way to better things.' The last words of J.M.W. Turner, that master-painter of light, were supposed to have been 'the Sun is God'. Such concerns were definitely in the air. Max Müller, who dominated the newly 'scientific' study of mythology in the 1860s and '70s, believed that the Sun was 'the chief burden of the myths of the Aryan race'. And, as we shall see later, solar physicists were beginning to argue the case for their own version of such myths.

On another occasion, Varley's accuracy was perhaps more practically, if indirectly, useful. Sometime around July 1822, when he went to Yarmouth to stay with the Turners, he decided to pay a visit to his friend John Sell Cotman, living nearby. For several months, Cotman had been in the throes of a severe nervous breakdown. As described in a letter of 5 October 1822 from Elizabeth Turner to her father, when Varley called, he was refused admittance by the maid, who told him that her master had already been given up by the doctors. He insisted, however, and upon entering the room said, 'Why Cotman, you're not such a fool as to think that you are going to die! Impossible, no such thing! I tell you there are yet twenty years for you yet to come.' Cotman's biographer writes that 'Varley's prophecy, based, as he claimed, on his astrological lore, came very near the truth, for Cotman lived for nineteen years and nine months after the prediction was made.'

The above stories are reasonably well authenticated. Others, less so, still fit the general pattern. For example, one story recounts that Varley was examining the nativity he had drawn up of a young lady about sixteen years old. He forecast marriage in a few years and the birth of one child. Then, stopping short, he said — and the manner, worth noting, is of someone perceiving something definite and even surprising — 'Hallo, what's this? a second marriage!' What he declined to relate, but did so privately to a friend, was his intimation that the second marriage would take place before the first had ended. In the event, the woman's first husband disappeared to Australia and, gathering after many years' enquiry that he was dead, she remarried. It turned out subsequently that her first husband was still alive, though now considered insane and incarcerated, in Australia.

What is the pattern of Varley's astrology that emerges from these stories? First, the frequency of his successes and their apparent unlikeliness stand out in any company. His successes are very impressive and, I argue below, such impressiveness was central to Varley's purpose. Second, his practice was highly predictive and specific. A far cry from any modern tendency to psychobabble, it more closely resembles the astrology of a medieval or seventeenth-century practitioner. Third, the events predicted, although precise, rarely seem avoidable; there is an air of inevitability. And many involve death or disaster. In these respects too, Varley's judicial astrology could be said to be typical of the subject in its classical or pre-modern age.

One must remember Varley's commitment to astrology as natural philosophy and natural law. In his view, as he wrote,

> astrology does not necessarily interfere with free will: for all astrology is nothing more than the experience and observation of coincidences, in which the astrologian is distinguished by a greater degree of knowledge and research, and a more methodical arrangement of facts and correspondence, than is possessed by our aunts and grandmothers, who are sybils in their way, and predict from certain appearances in the sky, fair or bad weather. Every man in the nation is daily imitating the practice of astrology, by anticipating what certain persons will do on certain occasions, from his knowledge of their usual habits and past actions. And if anyone, on looking at his watch, should predict that the great Tom of Lincoln would soon strike twelve, I do not imagine that Tom's free will to strike would in the least be affected by the prediction.

I am not suggesting that this view of the matter should be accepted entirely at its apparent face value. Like many of his contemporaries, Varley would have subsumed both divination and science under a common umbrella of systematic observation; whereas today, reading the same passage, we would assume a sharp distinction between the two. Bearing that in mind, I think Varley's predictions are better (if no more explicably) understood as divinations from omens — albeit a relatively stable, ordered and systematic approach to omens — than as simply matter-of-fact deductions from the phenomena. After all, even modern science, despite frequent claims to the contrary, does not really proceed like that. Nevertheless, it would be unfair to accuse Varley of hypocrisy, disguising a morbid or magical practice with claims of science. The sincerity of his belief cannot be doubted. Nor can his rigorous attention to symbolism, to which he himself undoubtedly would have attributed his own successes.

As for the larger meaning of his predictions or prophecies, it seems to me that they amounted to a metaphysical *trompe-l'oeil*, a way of saying: Look at the harmony and precision of the universe, of Nature, of Nature's god! The more spectacular and impressive they were, the more they were attempts, and probably often successful ones, to get the persons concerned — whether as the object of the prediction, or as its vicarious participants through hearing the story — to stop in their tracks, consider the handiwork of the gods and learn humility. In which case, there was not such a divide after all between the aesthetic imperative, in the broadest sense, of Varley's art and his astrology.

For centuries, astrologers have faced hostility from religious authorities, who disliked the competition from these unauthorized prophets. With the early nineteenth century, however, we are firmly in the modern period and the offended parties have changed somewhat. One who attacked Varley most bitterly was the science-writer and popularizer, Thomas Dick, in his book, *On the Improvement of Society by the Diffusion of Knowledge: or, An Illustration of the advantages which would result from a more general dissemination of rational scientific information among all ranks*. It was produced in association with the Society for the Diffusion of Useful Knowledge (SDUK), which was among the most determined opponents of astrology in the nineteenth century. Its tone of moral indignation, so necessary for the good imperialist, is typical of nineteenth-century attacks on astrology and is therefore worth quoting at some length:

> The greater part of the continent of America, the extensive plains of Africa, the vast regions of Siberia ... [and so on] still lie within the confines of mental darkness. On the numerous tribes which people those immense regions of our globe, neither the light of science nor of Revelation has yet shed its benign influence ... Even in Europe, where the light of science has chiefly shone, how narrow is the circle which has been enclosed by its beams! The lower orders of society on the continent, and even in Great Britain itself, notwithstanding the superior means of achievement they enjoy, are still miserably deficient ...

In particular, Dick bemoans

> those foolish notions, so fatal to the peace of mankind, which have been engendered by judicial astrology ... Even in this present day, and in the metropolis of the British Empire, this fallacious art is practised, and its professors are resorted to for judicial information, not only by the vulgar, but even by many in the higher spheres of life.

Who is to blame? One at least is 'Mr Varley, the prince of modern astrologers'. His 'success' (Dick cannot have meant his sales) 'is a proof, that strong efforts are still requisite to extirpate the superstition of astrology from the minds of many of our countrymen'.

As an example of the consequences of attending astrologers, Dick tells the story of a servant girl who responded to a notice advertising 'Mrs Smith, No. 49, Wentworth St., Dress Maker. Lawful questions resolved.' In answer to the girl's question — 'What sort of husband shall I have, and how soon shall I have him?' — Mrs Smith drew up an horary figure for the time of the question and foresaw 'a nice respectable tradesman, who should be a most tender husband' and six children for the happy parents. Soon after, however, the girl was caught borrowing her mistress's clothes and satin bonnet when she returned late from a night out. The astrologer's forecast was also found on a piece of paper on her person. As a result, she was 'brought to a watch-house', i.e. reformatory. Ruinous indeed — but at whose hands?

Dick was not alone. The Reverend William Harness used to declare that, in his case, Varley's predictions were entirely wrong. Another and more eminent critic was Augustus Frederick, the Duke of Sussex. Relations between him and his father, George III, were cool. The problem was the duke's liberal politics — parliamentary reform, abolition of the slave trade, Catholic emancipation and the advancement of the arts and sciences — in which connection he officiated as President of the Royal Society from 1830 until 1838. The duke was also active in freemasonry; initiated in 1798, he was elected head of the United Grand Lodge in 1813 and remained so until his death in 1843.

Neither his liberalism nor his freemasonry, however, interfered with the duke's habit of ridiculing Varley and astrology — asking, no doubt to an audience of appreciative smirks and titters, whether the stars could account for some corns with which he had lately been troubled. And why should it have been otherwise, unless we associate liberalism with liberal-democratic toleration and freemasonry with occultism? But in early Victorian England, we can do neither.

Despite this opposition, Varley enjoyed much favour in aristocratic circles. Doubtless he was an object of amusement, but he never refused an opportunity to bedazzle and instruct, nor, being impecunious, the offer of a free dinner. From 1818 until 1823, he was a regular guest at the Blessingtons' house, 11 St James's Square. The earl was no aristocrat of ancient lineage, but an immensely wealthy man recently ennobled. His young wife, Marguerite, Countess of Blessington — née Sally Power, from Cashel, County Tipperary — was then beginning a life-long quest for social pre-eminence. Nathaniel Parker Willis, a visiting American journalist, recorded his impressions in fulsome tones:

> admirable shape . . . her complexion (an unusually fair skin, with very dark
> hair and eyebrows) is of even a girlish delicacy . . . her features are regular,
> and her mouth, the most expressive of them, has a ripe fullness . . . Add to
> all this a voice merry and sad by turns, but always musical, and manners
> of the most unpretending elegance . . . and you have the prominent traits
> of one of the most lovely and fascinating women I have ever seen.

Aided by a daring that put her chief rivals, among them Lady Holland,
at some disadvantage, Lady Blessington soon established a varied and
glittering circle. On at least one occasion, Varley took Blake with him
to dine at the Blessingtons'. Among the visitors, on various occasions,
was Henry Brougham, the future lord chancellor and the chief mover
behind the SDUK (he and Varley probably encountered each other,
although we unfortunately do not know what transpired); Lord Byron;
the young Disraeli; Charles Dickens; and the *éminence grise* of the Victorian astrological and occult community, Edward George Earle Lytton
Bulwer, made the first Baron Lytton in 1838, and later usually known
merely as Sir Edward Bulwer-Lytton.

From the same visiting journalist, we know that Bulwer-Lytton was

> short, very much bent in the back, slightly knock-kneed and as ill-
> dressed a man for a gentleman as you will find in London . . . His head
> is phrenologically a fine one. His forehead retreats very much, but is very
> broad and well-marked, and the whole air is of decided mental superiority
> . . . He ran up to Lady Blessington with the joyous heartiness of a boy
> let out of school . . . A more good-natured, habitually smiling, nerveless
> expression could hardly be imagined. He was in the highest spirits.

Initially progressive in politics, Bulwer-Lytton supported the first Reform
Bill, but increasingly promoted landed and imperial interests, becoming
a Conservative member of Parliament in 1852 and a peer in 1866.
However, he was still better known as the author of some of the most
popular Victorian novels ever written, among them *The Last Days of
Pompeii*, *Zanoni*, *A Strange Story* and *The Coming Race*. Essential to
these books and a considerable part of their attraction was a sensational

pot-pourri of occultism and magic: supernatural forces, ceremonial magic, Rosicrucianism, Isis-worship, and a race of super-beings living under the Earth, to name but some of the ingredients. A favourite character was the elderly master, in one case also an artist, who initiates the author into the arcane mysteries.

Among the readers who devoured Bulwer-Lytton's works — and perhaps the first, although not the last, to treat them as literal truth — was the young Helena Petrovna Blavatsky, while visiting London for the first time in 1845. Later, in 1851, she caught a coveted glimpse of their author during the Great Exhibition at Crystal Palace. To what extent his books contributed directly to her own occult colossi *Isis Unveiled* and *The Secret Doctrine* is controversial, but after his death she enthused:

> No author in the world of literature ever gave a more truthful or more poetical description of these [spiritual] beings than Sir Edward Bulwer Lytton ... Now himself a *thing not of matter* but an *Idea of joy and light* ... whom many with reason believed to know more than he was prepared to admit in the face of a credulous public.

Bulwer-Lytton probably did know more of these things, in a personal capacity, than his readers guessed. Allowing for possible literary embellishment, he claimed to have first encountered divination as a young man, in the form of an uncannily perceptive gypsy-woman who 'read' his palm. The session ended thus:

> — Chut! Chut! but that new star thwarts you much.
> — What of the star?
> — I don't know what they call it. But it makes men fond of strange studies, and brings about crosses and sorrows that you never think to have.

The 'new star' was Uranus and with hindsight this description in both respects could certainly be said to be true. His youthful marriage was a life-long cross.

More impressively, in 1837 Bulwer-Lytton undertook to cast a geomantic figure as to the character and future career of Disraeli. His striking interpretation of the result was as follows:

> No figure I have drawn more surprises me than this. It is so completely opposed to what I myself should have augured ... He will bequeath a repute out of all proportion to the opinion now entertained of his intellect, even by those who think most highly of it. Greater honours, far more than he has acquired, are in store for him. His enemies, though active, are not persevering; his official friends, though not ardent, will yet minister to his success.

Bulwer-Lytton's son later confirmed that these conclusions 'were not suggested by my father's views, but in glaring opposition to them. The event, which verified his divination, contradicted his judgement.' I should add that his ability to permit a divinatory judgement to overrule or at least contradict his personal opinion bespeaks some degree of proficiency in that art.

There is little doubt that in this and all such matters Bulwer-Lytton's chief instructor was John Varley. Writing in 1894, A.T. Story remarked that the two men 'worked at astrology together, and in the occult machinery of the works named Bulwer is said to have been much indebted to suggestions given to him by the artist'. Certainly Varley's grasp of occultism and its various branches cannot be doubted, and when Lady Blessington moved to Gore House, Kensington — where she re-established her salon in 1836, some years after the death of her husband — both he and Bulwer-Lytton were often there together. Varley would speak at length to the party in Lady Blessington's library, illustrating points of doctrine with accounts of extraordinary experiences, both his own and those of others. Indeed, as Michael Sadleir described it,

> A craze for occultism seized on the company. Headed by Bulwer and Disraeli, they plunged into discussion and experiment. They listened entranced to Varley's stories of his extraordinary friend William Blake; they debated the pros and cons of witchcraft and spiritualism; they even tried their hands at crystal-gazing, with the help of a famous crystal given to their hostess by Nazim Pasha.

This Indian crystal would later reappear in the world of Victorian

astrology, where it achieved even greater notoriety. In 1849, threatened
by bankruptcy, Lady Blessington and her devoted but profligate partner
Alfred, Count d'Orsay, fled to Paris. She died later that same year and
from 7 May for twelve days the contents of Gore House went to auction.
(The house itself was pulled down a few years later in order to build the
Albert Hall.) Throngs of curious spectators, gloating rivals, melancholy
past acquaintances and avid buyers attended. Among them was a dealer
in curiosities with a shop in Brompton, whence Richard James Morrison,
better known as the aforementioned Zadkiel, departed with the crystal
a month or so later.

Astrologers and overt occultists were hardly the only people who
found precious stones compelling. Perhaps it was entirely coincidental,
but when Disraeli — who appreciated the importance of symbolism as
much as anyone — invented the Raj in 1858, with Queen Victoria as
its empress, he chose as its central symbol a great Indian diamond, the
Koh-i-noor, in her crown. Ten years later, Wilkie Collins gripped the
imagination of the entire British reading public with his yarn about
another Indian gem, this time with a curse on it, in the eponymous
The Moonstone.

In the autumn of 1842, Varley, aged 64 and still supporting a family,
was in desperate financial straits. He had been advanced £1,000 in
credit against a friend's scheme for a new design of carriage. When
it fell through, he was unable to honour his bills and a flurry of writs
were issued against both his goods and person. A lawyer's clerk serving
one of these took pity on Varley and hid him in his own home. It was
there that William Vokins found him, beset but still cheerful and working. Vokins settled his debts and moved him into his own home at 67
Margaret Street, off Cavendish Square. At around this time, however,
Varley caught a chill while sitting on the grass in the Chelsea Physic
Garden and sketching the cedar trees. His kidneys became inflamed and
he took to his bed. The doctor was called, but did not consider his case to
be very serious. The patient, however, disagreed. One day, his son Albert
visited him and sat down at his bedside. Around Varley on the bed lay his

almanacs and ephemerides, which he had been studying as usual. Albert expressed hopes for a speedy recovery, but his father replied, 'I shall not get better, my boy. All the aspects are too strong against me to recover.' And on 17 November he died.

Unsurprisingly, given the climate of opinion, Varley's reputation as an astrologer soon dwindled to the point where today few astrologers know of him except perhaps as a painter. Of course, the absence of surviving written material by Varley also contributed to his neglect. But the memory of him was kept alive by his predictions, some of which came true, in typically spectacular fashion, many years after his death. Whether correctly or not, Varley was widely supposed to have forecast the date of the death of William Collins, the eminent painter, in 1847. (Collins had been born very near Varley's residence in Great Titchfield Street.) And it is not surprising to hear from his grandson John that among other things Varley had foretold for his son Albert, when the latter was still a boy, was 'that at or about the age of sixty [i.e. in 1864] he would suffer from stone in the bladder, which was perfectly correct. He suffered very severely for about two years, and then quite recovered.'

That same year, Albert Varley was the executor to his cousin Paul Mulready, after the latter's sudden death. Looking through the surviving papers and correspondence, he came upon a letter; he read it, then handed it to his son John who was present. The letter, which Adrian Bury recorded, writing in 1946, was to Paul from his father William. It read as follows:

> 11 Fitzroy Street, Fitzroy Square
> With my foot in the grave and my eye on a better world, I now address you to remind you of what your uncle said concerning your future, [that] in your sixtieth year you would suffer from medical men and their ruffianly assistants. That I think is past. You had a brain fever from intense heat and vexatious circumstances and it was mistaken for insanity. At this period he said you must beware of rascally lawyers who would fleece you and then turn round and declare you insane and above

all you must avoid playing at Cricket or Boxing as you were likely to receive a Ball or a blow that might prove *fatal* and that from the hand of a friend or one nearly allied to you. Now I entreat you to avoid Boxing even in sport. If you get over the next six months you may have twenty happy years. It would be a cruel thing after a life of trouble to die when a prospect of comfort is before you. God bless you and prosper you, my dear boy.

April 19, 1864

Later that year, Paul went to watch some cricket practice with a friend at Kennington Oval. While chatting with his friend, the cricket ball in play struck his knee. Varley's grandson recalls:

The injury was, I believe, not very serious, but I heard it said that the medical treatment was quite wrong. I remember him being wheeled about in a bath-chair by his man-servant, and paid several visits to him at his house in South Kensington. He was cheerful, and I think at that time did not suffer much pain. He was, however, unable to walk or stand. Later on white swelling set in and an operation was necessary — his leg was amputated by the well-known surgeon, Holmes Coote. Two or three days later he died — I believe from shock to the system; but for this accident it is very probable that he would have lived for many years, as he was a man of great bodily strength and a wonderful constitution ... I understood my father to say that Paul had been born in my grandfather's house, and that the horoscope had been made at his birth, that is sixty years before the accident that caused death.

I would like to close with a different story, however. It is classic Varley, with a difference: a happy ending. It also embodies the problems that skill in an 'impossible' calling presents. Both Varley and Mulready were friends with another artist, A.W. Callcott. According to the story's sources, Richard and Samuel Redgrave:

A curious story used to be told among members of Callcott's family, and during the lifetime of both parties ... Varley asked Callcott to give him his exact age, and having obtained it, cast his nativity, sealed it up and gave it to Mulready, charging him to keep it safely until Callcott was fifty years old. The paper, it is said, was laid aside and forgotten until Callcott, then in his fiftieth year, wrote to Mulready, to invite him to his wedding, which was about to take place with Mrs Graham, the widow of Captain Graham. Mulready recollected Varley's sealed paper and his injunction, and took the document with him, opening it in the presence of the assembled company; the contents ran thus — 'Callcott will remain single until he is fifty, and then will marry and go to Italy.' As the painter really was to make a trip, shortly after his wedding, it was thought a wonderful coincidence.

But, they continue,

Over and over we have heard this tale told, with many other of Varley's wild fancies; but if our dates are accurate, Callcott was married on the twentieth of February 1827, his forty-eighth birthday, and started for Italy on the twelfth of May following, so that we have a false date, or Varley made a false prediction.

By this elegantly exhaustive logic — the resort of those, to quote Louis MacNiece, whose speech is 'cramped to Yea and Nay' — honour is saved. Although correct about Callcott's late marriage and a trip to Italy, Varley was two years out of reckoning; his forecast can therefore be appropriated by astrologers and ignored by sceptics with equal equanimity. But wonder cannot be coerced, and for their part astrologers themselves rarely approach Varley's standards. Even his direct hits missed their mark among those indisposed to share his own sense of the fittingness of fate. Grantley Berkeley remarked pityingly:

Poor Varley! I do not think a better-hearted fellow ever existed. If a man casts nativities, and predicts the consequent of individuals very often, it would be strange indeed if some of his guesses at the future did not occasionally prove true, precisely as is the case with dreams.

Varley's remains now lie in Kensal Green Cemetery; the headstone is no more, and his grave is unmarked. In one of history's levelling ironies, he shares the cemetery with his critic the Duke of Sussex, who was buried there a year later. Varley's house at 10½ Great Titchfield Street, too, has been replaced by an undistinguished modern office building, presently occupied by a property development company; and Broad Street, where he lived and where Blake was born, is now Broadwick Street. A blue plaque commemorates the poet; the building of his birth long gone, it is placed next to Crank's wholefood restaurant.

CHAPTER II

RAPHAEL: ENGLAND'S JUNIOR MERLIN

ALLOW ME TO INTRODUCE YOU TO Raphael, in his natural setting and his own words:

> It was night; the Moon shone gaily over tower and steeple, and brightly lit the vast metropolis: her refulgent beams illumined the nocturnal hemisphere with an unusual splendour, which streamed full in goodly rays upon the casement of the astrologer's study, where Raphael sat poring over the fates of Kings, Emperors, and distinguished individuals.
>
> ... a deep and awful silence reigned around, it was the hour of midnight ... the astrologer paused, and, struck with the ominous aspects of the time, proceeded to gaze upwards to the blue vault of heaven, in admiration of those myriad bright and shining orbs that lay expanded in an azure sea of celestial glory around him.

With this passage of the most purple prose, we pass from Varley's study in London, with its real enough twilight, curious books and bits of fruit pie, to a study mainly in the mind. And not just Raphael's mind for, through his pioneering efforts, the astrologer as Romantic magus, bearer of an ancient esoteric knowledge (or an incomprehensible legacy of superstition), became the dominant image of astrology in the age. Raphael's avidity to create this being, and with him a profitable and even respectable new niche in English society, required him to re-create his own identity too — beginning with his new name, adopted from that of the mystical Hebrew angel of Mercury. All in all, his programme contrasts strikingly with John Varley's directness and innocence. Varley may have been a far better astrologer, but the self-invented Raphael, in all his artful unauthenticity, was the genuine modern. As such, it was he who set the future course of modern astrology.

Raphael was born Robert Cross Smith, at 9.07 a.m. on 19 March 1795, in the village of Abbott's Leigh near Bristol. Probably of plebeian origins, he seems to have been largely self-educated. He soon moved to London, working initially as a junior clerk in Thames Street. In 1820 he married Sarah Lucas, by whom at the time of his death, as his contemporary, the astrologer Dixon, put it, 'he had six children, who are all living, and to add to the calamity, another in embryo'. The Smiths' home was at 5 (later and for longer, 75) Castle-Street East, just north of Oxford Street.

By all accounts Smith had a sensitive and melancholic temperament, the kind described a few decades later as 'neurasthenic'. Zadkiel, another astrologer, described him as 'slender and delicate; he was of a pale complexion, and had fine intelligent eyes, such as persons born under the sign Gemini [Raphael's ascendant] are generally observed to have ... The manners of Raphael were engaging, his soul was poetic, and his principles were in the highest degree philosophical.' But Dixon was less flattering. Discussing Smith's nativity, he lamented the imperfection of an aspect of Mercury to Saturn, which otherwise 'would have tended greatly to have arrested his too flighty imagination, and to have used less pompous diction ... ' Indeed, had not such a 'penchant for obscurity' been modified by another aspect,

> it would be difficult to say to what lengths this romantic passion for the marvellous would have carried him. He had the opportunity of becoming one of the first artists [i.e. astrologers] of the day, had he adhered to the principles of astrology; but his restless mind would not permit him to investigate sufficiently the merits of any one science, before his attention was immediately directed to the chimerical doctrines of some other; thus

his fluctuating mind never became fixed to any one object, even to the time of his death.

Astrology was the young Smith's longest love, however, and it seems to have had an immediate and powerful appeal for him. Given his taste for life's 'awful mysteries', combined with a somewhat fastidious nature, it is not hard to see why. Horoscopic astrology promises the ability to discern, and thereby vicariously participate in, the destinies of 'Kings, Emperors and distinguished individuals', all from the safety and comfort of a quiet study. It thus endows the astrologer with the seductive aura of an *éminence grise*, far from the vulgar hurly-burly of battle itself.

Smith's discovery of astrology and the occult was not only against the odds — for in the London of the 1820s they had nowhere near their later Victorian popularity — but he also pursued his chosen career tenaciously, despite the obstacles that lack of public recognition caused him. One reason was that unlike Varley, but like every other major astrologer in this period (and this was a crucial difference), Smith had no alternative source of income. He was therefore obliged to make astrology pay and, to a considerable extent from this time on, astrology can be seen as a strange amalgam resulting from the collision of ancient astrological tradition with the demands of modern market forces.

Not long after arriving in London, Smith struck up a friendship with George Graham, a balloonist whose miraculous survivals from his various disastrous aerial forays reliably drew large crowds throughout the 1820s and '30s. In keeping with this colourful persona, Graham was an equally enthusiastic student of the occult arts and he generously offered to sustain Smith while he launched his new career. (Mrs Smith's thoughts on this venture are unrecorded.) He probably also provided Smith's entry into the Stygian darkness of early Victorian occultism.

It is hard to say, being dark, whether that world was tiny or just well concealed, but, apart from Graham and the unmistakable figure of Varley, whom Raphael also knew, a few others can be discerned. One was John Denley, who appears in the introduction to Bulwer-Lytton's

Zanoni as the mysterious 'D---', the proprietor, like Denley, of an occult bookshop in Covent Garden. Denley provided Smith with more than one hoary occult manuscript and was usually waiting to buy up his remaindered books afterwards.

Denley's shop in Catherine Street (and later at the nearby 24 Brydges Place) was, Bulwer-Lytton admitted, once 'one of my favourite haunts'. In *Zanoni* he used it as the setting for his own fateful encounter with a Rosicrucian gentleman, presumably likewise drawn by 'the most notable collection, ever amassed by an enthusiast, of the works of Alchemist, Cabalist, and Astrologer'. Mysterious masters aside, however, there is no reason to doubt Bulwer-Lytton's description of the setting:

> The owner had lavished a fortune in the purchase of unsaleable treasures. But old D--- did not desire to sell. It absolutely went to his heart when a customer entered his shop; he watched the movements of the presumptuous intruder with a vindictive glare, he fluttered around him with uneasy vigilance; he frowned, he groaned, when profane hands dislodged his idols from their niches. If it were one of the favourite sultanas of his wizard harem that attracted you, and the price named were not sufficiently enormous, he would not unfrequently double the sum. Demur, and in brisk delight he snatched the veritable charmer from your hands; accede, and he became the picture of despair . . .

Another fixture was Francis Barrett, a self-described Rosicrucian who was the centre of an occult group at his home, 99 Norton Street, Mary-le-Bonne (i.e. Marylebone). The Order of the Rosy Cross was a secret magical order, first mentioned in the seventeenth century, about which little is known. Perhaps a love of wonders, whether aeronautical or supernatural, was the link between these two activities, or a desire to rise above mundane reality; or even, it has been unkindly suggested, a fondness for hot air. At any rate, Barrett was another enthusiastic balloonist. He also knew Denley and, like Smith, almost certainly obtained most of his source materials from him.

Smith's first offering, written with Graham and published by Denley, was *The Philosophical Merlin* of 1822, which presented itself as the 'translation of a valuable manuscript in the possession of Napoleon Bonaparte'. In fact, most of it was borrowed from Barrett's *The Magus, or Celestial Intelligencer* published in 1801. Far from 'Being A Complete System of Occult Philosophy', in the words of the subtitle, it was anything but systematic: a sprawling *mélange* of natural and ceremonial magic, alchemy, Hermeticism, astrology, the Cabbala and numerology quarried in turn from the mythical Hermes Trismegistus, Paracelsus, John Dee, Cornelius Agrippa, Ebenezer Sibly and older astrological authorities. *The Magus* continued to provide Smith, Bulwer-Lytton and others with a rich vein for future works. Public response to *The Philosophical Merlin* was, however, distinctly underwhelming, and most of the print run was remaindered.

Undeterred, Smith next became editor of a weekly periodical, *The Straggling Astrologer*, a few weeks after its initial appearance in June 1824. He is identified only as one of a mysterious group called 'the Mercurii', whose members 'are at present but few and select . . . The place where these scientific gentlemen at present meet must, as yet, remain a secret.' There were also contributions from 'H.R.H. The Princess Olive of Cumberland', also known as Mrs Oliva Serres, who claimed to be the unacknowledged daughter of George III's brother. Despite such attractions, *The Astrologer of the Nineteenth Century* — as it was later rechristened — collapsed after twenty-two issues. Smith's new publisher, Walter Charleton Wright, then parsimoniously bound and reissued the remaining copies as a book of that title in 1825. Here, for the first time, Smith makes his appearance as 'Raphael, the Metropolitan Astrologer'.

Wright and Smith then agreed on a second edition, considerably expanded and with lavish colour plates; it appeared (described as the seventh edition!) later that same year. Subtitled 'The Master Key of Futurity, and Guide to Ancient Mysteries, being a Complete System of Occult Philosophy', *The Astrologer of the Nineteenth Century* now included advice on invoking spirits, 'Curious Secrets' and 'Anecdotes of the Dead and Terrific Legends', and a section on astrology that stretched from 'Wonderful Prophecies by Celebrated Astrologers' to discussions of the nativities of that perennial subject of interest, the royal family. It was dedicated 'To the Author of Waverley', i.e. Sir Walter Scott, to whose novels Smith optimistically attributed 'the intense interest now so generally evinced relative to . . . "the Occult Sciences".' Sad to say, despite this hoped-for interest, Wright became temporarily bankrupt. Copyright passed to another publisher, Knight and Lacey, who quickly suffered the same fate, and the ill-starred *Astrologer of the Nineteenth Century* was finally sold off to yet another London bookseller.

In addition to 'Raphael', Smith now also identified himself as 'Merlinus Anglicus, Junior', i.e. England's Junior Merlin. This appellation had once belonged to the most famous astrologer of seventeenth-century England, William Lilly — a reference and a claim lost on most of Smith's readers, although not on other astrologers. However, the contrast between his own struggles to survive and Lilly's success almost two centuries earlier is striking. It was underlined by Smith's attempt in 1825 to launch yet another astrological periodical, this time a monthly, entitled *Urania; or, The Astrologer's Chronicle, and Mystical Magazine*. The publisher was again John Denley. Beginning on a slightly defensive note — proofs of astrology, it was declared, 'will be sufficiently authenticated to attract the attention of those who are *believers* in the doctrines of sidereal and occult influence, and to none other do we write' — it lasted only one year. The fact was that the public did not yet include sufficient 'believers', even in the broadest sense, to support a popular astrological publication.

By now, Smith was understandably discouraged. In 1826, he resolved to abandon astrology and open a coffee-house in Poland Street. However, he was unable to raise sufficient capital for the project. At this point, together with Wright, who was now back in business, Smith decided on perhaps a final attempt to succeed at what he knew best. This time the plan was for an annual periodical entitled *The Prophetic Messenger*. The content was to be entirely astrological and/or occult, spiced with not only supernatural sensationalism but also a great deal of prediction, some of it daringly precise. Above all, it contained the innovation of astrological forecasts for every day of the coming year. The *Messenger* thus differed significantly from both its ancestors (including yet another failed publication of the same name, that limped along from 1820 to 1826) and its possible competitors, such as the hoary and more down-market *Moore's Vox Stellarum*.

The first issue appeared on 10 November 1826 and this time something clicked. It is hard to say why, but several factors must have contributed: Smith's polished journalistic skills; the new format; and greater receptivity on the part of the London reading public. *The Prophetic Messenger* was an instant success: the first run sold out immediately. A month later, Wright ordered a reprint, adding in a gratified note to the printers that rarely had his efforts as a publisher been '*so quickly* and *so amply* rewarded; one thousand copies have been disposed of to the London booksellers, to whom, as *gentlemen* and *commercial auxiliaries* I am particularly indebted.' A few years later, Wright claimed sales of 8,500 for the 1831 edition of *The Prophetic Messenger*.

Who bought and read the new almanac? Probably few of its buyers were already members of the considerable constituency (around 270,000 copies annually at this time) for *Moore's*. This, with its simplified astrology combined with other matters of more general interest — tides, annual fairs and general political commentary — had a loyal following among both rural labourers and the new urban working classes. The astrological detail of *The Prophetic Messenger*, as well as its rather overblown occult romanticism, would have been unlikely to appeal to such readers.

At the other end of the social spectrum, an upper-class prejudice against astrology still held sway. This had been inherited from astrologers' prominence in the sectarian strife of the middle and late seventeenth century, when for a while 'the world turned upside down.' Astrologers continued to be viewed by the allies and heirs of those subsequently restored to the top as vulgar and ignorant 'enthusiasts'.

It seems that Smith's most adventurous new readers came from the increasingly prosperous and powerful middle classes, people once aptly described as 'semi-erudite' — in other words, those sufficiently educated to hunger for quite complex ways in which to understand or enrich their lives, but not so learned that they were willing to confine themselves to the customary sustenance of religion, natural philosophy and polite literature. Indeed, there is a case for saying that those traditional guides had largely failed Smith's readers, who were therefore ready to seek out stronger meat in their search for instruction in life's mysteries. And mysteries, of course, were Smith's *métier*.

Ironically, for they would have found each other uncongenial company, some of his readers were probably the same sort of people who found solace in the Oxford Movement, an attempt to return to the theologically sanctioned mysteries of Catholicism which shook the Anglican Church from 1833 and during the 1840s. Both movements were reponding to a sense of loss and uncertainty resulting from the successes of secularism, whether as political radicalism, philosophical utilitarianism or science.

On the strength of *The Prophetic Messenger*, various publishers commissioned Raphael — which, respecting his new identity, I shall now call him — to produce more books. The first was his only serious astrological textbook, *A Manual of Astrology*, which was published in 1828. One of its example horoscopes notes that he commenced writing it at exactly noon on 4 August 1826. Whatever he saw in the map (and although overall quite a positive one, an astrologer would say it is distinctly unpromising with respect to publishing), this time Raphael took the precaution of selling his copyright for £100 in advance. This was wise as, not surprisingly for such a detailed and technical work, sales were poor.

Otherwise, the *Manual* is notable only for having introduced the case of Mr Samuel Hemmings, supposedly born at the same time and date as George III, and in a nearby place. According to Raphael, based on a story widely reported in the popular press in February 1820, Hemmings went into business in October 1760, the very month that the king acceded to the throne, they were both married on 8 September 1761, and even died on the same day, 29 January 1820. Here, as so often, we must exercise Keats's 'negative capability' and refrain from any 'irritable reaching after fact and reason'. We do not know the origin of the newspaper reports themselves, but Raphael seized on them as demonstrating the idea that the stars confer destiny commensurate with the circumstances of the person concerned; and the story, through him, has survived to cheer and instruct astrologers down to the twentieth century.

More typical of Raphael's output in this period was *The Royal Book of Fate, Destiny and Foreknowledge*, published in 1829, 'which, without writing or calculations of any kind, contains four thousand and ninety answers to sixty-four questions of the most important subjects of human life', such as the somewhat plaintive, 'Shall the enquirer ever be rich?' Raphael claimed that he had purchased his original manuscript (of great antiquity, naturally) from Denley. Other books, reflecting a publishing strategy easily discernible from their titles, included *The Royal Book of Dreams*; *Raphael's Witch!!! or The Oracle of the Future*; and *The Familiar Astrologer: An Easy Guide to Fate, Destiny and Foreknowledge*. Most were published by Wright, whose ambitions were evident from the extended title of *Raphael's Sanctuary of the Astral Art: Being a Book for the Boudoir, Drawing-Room Table, and Evening Parties* ... This consisted of a geomantic divinatory game, beginning with the random drawing of dots on a piece of paper and ending with something rather like a simplified Tarot-card layout. There was a perfunctory nod to astrology in the interpretation of the final arrangement. It must have infuriated serious astrologers to have, in the words of Dixon, their 'rational and valuable science ... confounded with the thing called by certain persons Popular Astrology'.

But Raphael's heresy was vindicated, at least commercially. Just like their modern heirs — the countless popular occult and psychological manuals for self-knowledge and self-help, written with endless variations on a precise formula and beckoning from racks in bookshops, stationers and airports — these works sold well and saw many more editions later in the century. For the first time, Raphael was making money. However, while that must have been gratifying, it left unscratched a perennial itch that afflicts nearly all astrologers, then and now: the desire for respectability.

Actually, this need has two facets; one, the respect of one's astrological colleagues, looks inward; while the other, the respect of 'society', looks out. Regarding the first, Dixon's obituary of Raphael remarked that, 'In professing the science of *geomancy* and *magic*' — which of course he was obliged to do, in order to develop and exploit the new market for middle-class occcultism — 'Raphael incurred many enemies among his *astrological* friends . . . indeed, I have often heard Raphael say, "He wished he had never troubled himself with the study of these sciences to the extent he had, as he felt certain the truth of them was very problematical."' More to the point, Raphael's astrological peers undoubtedly felt they already had their hands full in contending with the usual religious and scientific criticism, without having magic added to their load. Of course, they may well also have envied his success.

The respect of society was an even greater concern. Raphael's *Companion to the Prophetic Messenger* opens with a rhetorical flourish which reveals the identity of his oppressors: 'Yes, kind reader, Raphael, in defence of Astrology, dares to the field alike the gnarling critic, the morose bigot, the phantastical literary fop of the fashionable book-world . . . ' Hence his attempt to go straight to the top, so to speak, in a story entitled 'A Remarkable Visit to the Author' — which certainly reads like a fantasy — in his *Prophetic Messenger* for 1832. It is worth quoting at some length:

> It was late in the dreary dusk of an autumnal eve, in the year 1828, that the *Astrologer* had newly trimmed his lamp, and sat down to serious contemplation of an astrological problem . . . when a furious ringing of the bell belonging to the study, and a simultaneous loud and hasty knocking at the door of his residence announced a visitor — one who was apparently little gifted with the virtue of patience; for, scarcely deigning to wait the announcement of his name and business, the intruder entered with an air of nonchalance and self-conceit, that told of his being something more than one of ordinary rank.
>
> He entered the Astrologer's study, and took, almost without bidding, a seat . . . the Stranger addressed him, and, in a tone of mild and gentlemanly politeness, requested the favour of the Astrologer's attention to his 'future Destiny'.

... the Astrologer drew forth his Tables, consulted his Ephemeris, and cast the Horoscope, or figure of the heavens for the hour and minute of the enquiry, according to the established rules of the sidereal art. But astonishment and awe quickly pervaded his countenance; for the *Radix* before him was indeed singular . . . But his reveries were cut short by the Stranger, who anxiously enquired . . . 'What good or bad fortune the stars had allotted him?'

'As to the first,' replied Raphael, 'I behold before me the certain testimonials of one who has basked smoothly in the gay retinue and smiles of fortune — who has perchance travelled, sojourned, and seen countless multitudes — who has wealth, power and fortune at his beck and bidding . . . '

'*It is such as you have said,*' replied the Stranger; 'I give you full credence for the **future**, since you have revealed the irrefragable past. But *apropos*, I would have you, Raphael, read a more deep sentence in the page of fate — *What say you of my life?*'

'As to that particular,' replied Raphael, 'sorry indeed am I to be the prophet of **evil**; from the too sure and fatal configurations here congregated before me, which are too many to tire you with the technical enumeration, I grieve to announce but a brief career, indeed, to the present inquirer.'

'*How Brief, say you?*' eagerly demanded the Stranger. To answer this question more faithfully, the Astrologer once more consulted the horoscope, in hopes also to see, if possible, some sign of mitigation to the impending calamity. But in vain: no friendly ray interposed to stay the fell and ireful aspects . . . The Astrologer, with unfeigned reluctance and grief of mind, announced that **Death was foretold** within the short space of two years!

'*Brief, indeed!*' remarked the Stranger. 'The view, Raphael, you have afforded me into futurity, I must confess, is of no cheering kind; but, as it becomes all to ponder well on our finite existence, I cannot but thank you for the results of your calculation. But one more word ere we separate; shall my posterity flourish?'

'Of *that*,' replied the Astrologer, 'rest assured . . . Moreover, I perceive

OMENS OF MIGHTY CHANGES as connected with your name and lineage!'

The stranger seemed more than usually pleased with this prediction; and in warm and friendly terms, proceeded to compliment the Astrologer; expressing his ardent conviction that the 'stars spoke truth', and that 'Astrology was veritably a *noble science.*' He shortly afterwards took leave . . . however, previous to leaving the Astrologer's residence, he left, either by accident or design, an enamelled costly card, from which the real station and title of the visitor was manifest. It was even as Raphael had foreseen, he was a man of *the highest rank in the kingdom*! . . . and as to the *fulfilment* of the horoscope, the reader need only be told, that the visitor was no other than his late Majesty **George the Fourth**.

As contemporary readers would have appreciated, George IV had died on 26 June 1830. At this point, Raphael was clearly just hitting his stride. Earlier editions of *The Prophetic Messenger* had merely warned (for example) that May 1831 'will be a month of *disasters . . . One of an illustrious family is troubled or afflicted*; something remarkable may happen to a Princess, or Noble Lady; a great man dies, and there is *evil news* from foreign parts.' But at 4.15 p.m. on 26 February 1832 — only thirty-six years old, and just at the point of achieving real professional success — Raphael himself died. He was buried nine days later in the vault of St Gregory's, on the south side of St Paul's Cathedral.

His health had long been delicate and his nemesis was 'consumption', i.e. tuberculosis. According to his widow, speaking later to Dixon, he 'was scarcely ever free from sickness long together, had but an indifferent appetite at the best of times, and during the last winter [was] scarcely able to attend to his astrological business . . . ' Raphael left her £600 and an immediate stream of overly solicitous callers offering their services in continuing *The Prophetic Messenger*.

One was Dixon himself. We know very little about him, apart from his birth data: conscientiously recorded, as befits a good astrologer, as 8.58 a.m. on 28 March 1795, probably in London. Dixon claimed 'a long acquaintance with Raphael', although his one previous publication

— a failed periodical which appeared in 1824–5, *The Spirit of Partridge* — revealed him to be a severe astrological purist (just like his journal's namesake, the astrologer John Partridge), who criticized Raphael for loose eclecticism. When Dixon overcame his scruples, however, and called upon Mrs Smith concerning *The Prophetic Messenger*, he found he had been anticipated. To his chagrin, she explained that upon Raphael's death, two young men, formerly pupils, had immediately offered to produce next year's issue: namely John Palmer, then working in a chemist's in the West End, assisted by one P. Moody, a messenger in the House of Lords. Dixon records a letter from the latter to Mrs Smith, peremptorily objecting 'to a mask being taken of Smith's face — *because it will give his death too great a publicity at present* — the full grounds I stated last night'.

Although Palmer later claimed that he had been 'much addicted to the occult sciences' since the age of fifteen, Dixon was probably right that his and Moody's commercial instincts far outstripped their grasp of astrology. But Dixon could hardly have been surprised over their plan to continue to edit *The Prophetic Messenger* under the name of Raphael. This was a well-known strategy for astrological almanacs, which had already resulted in astounding longevity for late seventeenth-century astrologers like Partridge and Francis Moore. In this way, dynastic lineages of popular astrologers appeared, almost as a parody of the official royal succession. Knowing what was at stake, Dixon was undoubtedly bitter at having been pipped at the post by Palmer, who duly became the second of no less than six Raphaels in all. Dixon's revenge was to produce *The True Prophetic Messenger for 1833* (published by John Denley), 'in order to prevent the dissemination of such trash as cannot fail to emanate from the hands of those who have yet to learn their ABC in astrology'. Its title-page, however, proclaims its author too as Raphael! After this, however, Dixon disappears.

The unseemly scramble to acquire the rights to Raphael's *The Prophetic Messenger* was driven by the existence of a ready new market for low-cost publications among the middle classes, together with new means of producing them cheaply: inexpensive paper, stereotyping and above all the steam-press. The perception of this commercial opportunity was widely shared, extending from Raphael and his successors and, to give him credit, Walter Charleton Wright to another equally shrewd writer and publisher, Charles Knight. Knight was bitterly anti-astrological, however, and he chose 1828 to put out the first *British Almanac*. Issued under the aegis of the Society for the Diffusion of Useful Knowledge, this publication was explicitly intended to put the old astrological almanacs such as *Old Moore's* out of business. But so too, to an extent, was *The Prophetic Messenger*.

The tussle between Raphael and Knight was part of a wider struggle for the minds and hearts of the literate labouring and lower-middle classes, in which 'respectable' publishers saw an opportunity to turn a profit by replacing the old radical and plebeian 'pauper presses', at the same time as converting new readers to their own points of view. England in the late 1820s and '30s saw an intense political struggle between radicals, Whigs and Tories, culminating in the first Reform Act of 1832 which extended the franchise by about fifty per cent. Particularly in the 1830s, control of London was virtually up for grabs. 'Useful knowledge' in this context of uncertainty carried a heavy political freight, being essentially code for the attempt by middle-class reformers to defend secularism and democracy from the dangerously open-ended interpretation given them by plebeian radicals. At the same time, the reformers also had to fight the Tory, aristocratic and Anglican resistance personified at the time by the Duke of Wellington.

Raphael's Prophetic Messenger continued to appear every year, through both Reform and the subsequent reaction. It was still published by Wright and edited by 'Raphael', initially using his old address of 75 Castle-Street East. Palmer continued in this capacity until his death in 1837, when one Medhurst took over as Raphael III. He was followed in 1853 by Wakeley, who was in turn succeeded the following year by R.V. Sparkes. Finally, after Sparkes's death in 1875, Robert T. Cross became the sixth and last known Raphael in 1876. At twenty-five, he was, along with Palmer, the youngest editor yet, and claimed to have begun studying astrology even earlier, at the age of twelve. Born in East Anglia, he came to London at fifteen and worked in an engineer's office for the next seven years. Cross later admitted, 'I have tried many things, but all have ended in failure and loss. In Astrology, however, I have succeeded beyond my expectations . . . ' He lasted until his death in 1923, the longest-running Raphael of all. Throughout, the tried-and-tested format continued to be followed. To pick a later example at random, the edition for 1850 notes, in a characteristic tone of edgily bluff confidence, 'To put Downing-street on the alert, we need only hint that in the month of June, "Jupiter quartiles Herschel".' Indeed!

Circulation figures are difficult to establish, but during Cross's time as Raphael, annual sales for the *Prophetic Almanac* (as it was renamed in 1840) reached about 100,000. By the end of the century, estimates varied from 162,000 to nearly 200,000. But that is not the end of the story. Although the present *Raphael's Astrological Almanac* is a rather diminished publication compared to its innovative ancestor, it still appears every year, and copyright apparently still belongs to members of the Cross family. *Raphael's Ephemeris* is also published annually and lists that year's planetary positions and aspects. A well-thumbed copy for the current year is owned by virtually every practising modern British astrologer, but few have ever stopped to wonder who Raphael was, or what they might owe him.

CHAPTER III

ZADKIEL: ASTROLOGY ON TRIAL

THE YEAR 1795 PRODUCED A VINTAGE crop of astrologers. In addition to Raphael and Dixon, someone else born that year not only came to dominate astrology in mid-Victorian England, but also frequented the drawing-rooms of some of its leading nobility and gentry. As the foremost representative of his art, however, he also became an object of scorn and derision in the pages of the *Athenaeum*, *The Times* and other leading organs of the establishment. He probably felt this sort of attention to be better than none. Commenting afterwards on the nativity of Zadkiel, as he was best known, one astrologer and sometime colleague remarked, 'Herschel rising with Regulus quite described the man's eccentric character . . . a stout, burly man — self-confident and combative.' In short, where Raphael had been retiring, Zadkiel was pugnacious. In the course of a long life, he soon eclipsed the former in fame and notoriety. That seems only fair, for in his style, energy and self-esteem, Zadkiel was a quintessentially Victorian man.

Richard James Morrison was born at 9.58 a.m. on 15 June in Edmonton, North London. His family background was genteel, with a tradition of naval and colonial service. He joined the Royal Navy at the age of eleven, and in the next nine years saw action in the Mediterranean against the French. After serving aboard the cruiser *Spartan*, he was decorated for bravery and promoted to lieutenant commander in 1815. Two years later, he retired on half-pay and served in the coastguard. In 1827, he married Sarah Mary Paul, the daughter of an Ango-Irish baronet, in Waterford; they had nine children before she died in 1849. He married again soon after her death and yet again after the death of his second wife.

Morrison seems to have taken up the study of astronomy and astrology soon after retiring from active duty. He had a distinctly personal approach to the former, which he outlined in such books as *The Solar System As It Is, and Not As It Is Represented*. His system was basically that of the sixteenth-century astronomer Tycho Brahe: i.e. with the Sun and Moon moving around the Earth and the other planets revolving around the Sun. But he added refinements of his own, maintaining, for example, that the Sun travels through space at 99,897 miles per hour, and is only 365,006 miles distant from the Earth. (The modern consensus is roughly 155 miles per second and 93 million miles respectively.) His books, always identified as by Lieutenant R.J. Morrison, R.N., received politely baffled reviews in journals from the *Athenaeum* to the *Liverpool Daily Post*. He also lectured on the subject to 'nearly 1,000 persons at Manchester', and on 24 March 1858 at the London Mechanics' Institute. However, the British Association refused to take any notice of him, which only confirmed his already low opinion of the experts.

The ruling passion of Morrison's life, however, was astrology. By 1824, he was a member of Raphael's occult group the Mercurii, but in 1831 he became Raphael's commercial competitor. Inspired by the success of the latter's *Prophetic Messenger*, Morrison issued his own version, *The Herald of Astrology*, for the following year. On its title-page, he makes his first appearance as 'Zadkiel, Tao Tse', followed, startlingly, to modern eyes, by a swastika. In so doing, Morrison had two intentions. One was to proclaim his existence as an astrologer while protecting his personal social standing — an ambition in which he was to be not entirely successful. The other was to display, to those in the know, his occult credentials: Zadkiel is the Cabbalistic name of the angel of Jupiter, the planet of wisdom; Tao Tse refers to the semi-historical founder of Taoism in fourth-century B.C. China; and the swastika was a metaphysical symbol in several cultures long before the Nazis adopted it.

Although *Zadkiel's Almanac* (as it was renamed in 1836) was modelled on that of Raphael, it bore the unmistakable stamp of its editor's larger-than-life personality. It also significantly undercut the price of its rival, and within a few years was outselling it. The annual sales grew steadily, from 22,000 copies in 1849, to nearly 32,000 in 1851, and to 44,000 ten years later. The obligatory textbook appeared in 1833: *The Grammar of Astrology, containing All Things Necessary for Calculating a Nativity*; this was followed two years later by an edited and annotated version of William Lilly's seventeenth-century classis *Christian Astrology*, which Zadkiel retitled *An Introduction to Astrology*. By then, his course was firmly set. He moved from Liverpool to Gloucestershire, where he conducted public discussions of astrology in Cheltenham and Gloucester, and charged the natives £10, not an inconsiderable sum, to calculate and interpret a nativity.

In the first of a life-long exchange of polemics, these activities were attacked in 1838 by T. H. Moody, a guardian of the faith and morality in Cheltenham, in a book called *A Complete Refutation of Astrology . . . in Reply to the Arguments of Lieutenant Morrison and others*. Moody noted gloomily that 'this system of imposture has lately been gaining ground in the British Empire'; he hoped 'that the present work may, in some degree, be instrumental in checking its progress'. His principal touchstone was biblical chapter and verse, condemning astrology as magic and divination, and modestly concluding 'It is not I who anathematize Astrologers: the word of God does this; and I proclaim the fact for the instruction and warning of the ignorant and unwary: it is charity to warn man of his danger . . . '

In fact, Zadkiel was in greater danger. In 1844, J. Bradshaw, an astrologer in Manchester, was convicted of fortune-telling and imprisoned for a month. This rang alarm bells with professional astrologers throughout the country. Their reaction can only be understood in the light of an earlier incident. In 1813, Thomas White, the author of an astrological textbook entitled *The Celestial Intelligencer*, was living in the Isle of Wight. He was approached by a police informer, who asked him for a reading and then paid with marked money. White was promptly arrested, his books and papers were seized and he was convicted under the Vagrancy Act for 'pretending or professing to tell Fortunes'. He died after three months in Winchester gaol.

Such prosecutions were not always successful; in the year that Bradshaw was arrested, the case against an astrologer in Bromley was abandoned and another in Rochdale won an appeal. None the less, these prosecutions were actively sought by the constabulary and judiciary, using paid informers to entrap the astrologer, and the penalty was usually severe: a prison sentence of up to three months, accompanied or followed by hard labour. Nor was an appeal usually permitted.

Understandably alarmed by the brutality of Bradshaw's treatment, Zadkiel reacted to his arrest by forming a 'British Association for the Advancement of Astral Science &c., and the Protection of Astrologers'. By 1845, he claimed to have 107 subscribers. No more is heard of it, but this was only the opening shot in Zadkiel's protracted struggle to change the law by advancing the cause of astrology, and vice versa. In the course of that struggle, the issue of the respectability or otherwise of astrology and of the man himself grew perilously entwined.

In 1846, Zadkiel moved to west London. He quickly became involved in the current passion for mesmerism or animal magnetism, later and more respectably known as hypnosis, as well as phrenology, the art or science of reading character by means of the shape and structure of the head. Zadkiel began conducting his own experiments by putting people into mesmeric trances and attended public demonstrations and discussions of the subject. At one such meeting in 1847, he was pointed out to a young solicitor attending out of curiosity, Christopher Cooke. It was a fateful encounter for Cooke. We may be grateful for it, although Cooke himself eventually was to regret it, for he is our most conscientious source of information about Zadkiel's career over the next decade and a half.

Educated at Harrow, Cooke was called to the bar in 1844. He lived with his mother at 2 Upper Grosvenor Street, a well-to-do address, and practised at 12 Southampton Buildings, Chancery Lane. His interest in Zadkiel, kindled at the public meeting, quickened after reading a copy of his *The Horoscope* for 1841, which explained the connections between astrology and phrenology: for example, that through a knowledge of zodiacal physiognomy, derived from Varley, a person's rising sign may be ascertained by his face and head. Cooke next bought and read Zadkiel's *Introduction to Astrology*; and finally, as a test, he sent in £10 and his birth data for a reading, sight unseen. The results apparently impressed him, although not so much as when, he later wrote,

> I applied for a reply to a horary question upon a particular matter, which was verified in such a singular manner, that the circumstance impressed me forcibly; and although I had, during the course of my two years' experience, found much general truth in the principles of astral science, I had never before experienced so pointedly the truth of such principles; and the circumstance which happened caused me to reflect deeply at the time of its occurrence — viz., the evening of Oct. 19, 1851 . . .

He felt obliged to conclude that 'Astrology was — the truth.'

Cooke's conviction gradually overpowered his caution. Zadkiel himself seemed to him 'a man of education, fair position in society — bearing in mind his illegal pursuit . . . Also, a good linguist, well versed in Hebrew and in the knowledge of ancient astronomy.' But the deciding factor seems to have been Cooke's irrepressible sense of truth and fair play, assisted by considerable naîvety. 'I could scarcely take up the newspaper,' he wrote, 'without seeing some stupid or malicious remark to the effect that the whole subject was fraud and meriting contempt.' Yet, in the light of his experience of astrology's truth, 'It seemed to me that this knowledge, properly applied, must at once abolish the notion of atheism, and necessarily destroy the dreary dreams of the materialist. Here was the Creator acting upon the created by means of the stars as His instruments, millions of miles away!' Cooke also thought that astrology held much practical promise. Together with phrenology, it could be used to match people's abilities and vocations, and instigate preventative education for those whose nativities showed a propensity for anti-social behaviour. This would result in 'much public benefit, and tend to increase public prosperity and to diminish public crimes'.

The immediate stumbling block in Cooke's view, both as a partisan and as a solicitor, was Section 4 of the Vagrancy Act. Zadkiel agreed, and the whole issue was soon brought to a head by the Copestick affair. Francis D. Copestick was an astrologer practising from his own house in Bath. He had also issued a little almanac from the 1830s and was a well-known local character. In December of 1851, a client seeking his advice turned out to be Captain Duff of the Bath police, in plain clothes. Copestick was arrested and his books and papers impounded, and on 10 January 1852 he was sentenced, under the terms of the Vagrancy Act, to a month's imprisonment with hard labour. The judge refused to hear Copestick's evidence in his own defence or to allow an appeal.

There were at least three similar prosecutions in 1851–3 — in Gloucester, Wakefield and Cambridge — but they were scarcely noted by the press or public. A rare exception was the *Sun*, whose liberal editor, Charles Kent, condemned Copestick's conviction as an invasion of privacy and natural justice. In his editorial of 19 January 1852, Kent wrote of astrology, 'erroneous let us still continue to regard it; but, at any rate, let it not be repressed by measures so very despicable, so wholly un-English . . . '

Cooke later remarked of Copestick's magistrate, truly, no doubt, that he 'was not generally unfair in his decisions, and his conduct upon this occasion was evidence of the extreme dislike which persons in his position have for the subject of Astrology'. Inflamed by this injustice, Cooke wrote to Zadkiel offering him a letter for his *Almanac for 1853* defending Copestick. The letter duly appeared, signed 'Lex'. In it, he pointed out that whereas someone like Copestick was singled out to be persecuted in Bath, a phrenologist or animal magnetist would go unmolested, 'and an Electro-biologist might have played his pranks there with impunity'.

Zadkiel had already resolved to petition Parliament to amend the Vagrancy Act, by excluding enfranchised householders from its terms. Accepting Cooke's offer of an article, therefore, Zadkiel seized the opportunity to involve him further: here was a chance to obtain legal advice concerning the terms of the petition. So, during March and April of 1852 at his smart terraced house at 1 Milborne Grove in Fulham, Zadkiel met with Cooke, together with another astrological man of law, William Sharp Cross.

Born near Liverpool at 5.10 a.m. on 1 August 1811, Cross was a sixth Wrangler at Cambridge — i.e. in the first class of the mathematical tripos — before becoming a successful barrister. Unlike Cooke, however, he had the good sense to keep his astrological interests strictly private. His sole publication, apart from various articles under the *nom de plume* of 'Scrutator', was an anonymous book in 1849 entitled *Reasons for Belief in Judicial Astrology; Comprising some Advice to Students, and Remarks on the Dangerous Character of Popish Priestcraft*. It was generally considered to be eccentric, even by other astrologers. After Cross died in 1861, Cooke described him as 'A legal character of much talent but tinged apparently with fatalism'.

Having hammered out the exact form of the petition, Zadkiel turned to exerting influence. Ten years earlier, as Morrison, he had been elected to the council of a short-lived London Meteorological Society; its president was Robert Grosvenor, a leading Whig politician and the future Baron Ebury. With Grosvenor as an intermediary, Zadkiel had also presented royal horoscopes and copies of his *Almanac* to Prince Albert in the early 1840s, although such attentions were soon found to be importunate; in 1847, Zadkiel forbore, unusually for him, to comment on the nativity of the queen, explaining that 'I was informed, from a high quarter, that my predictions had given some uneasiness to a personage for whom I have no other feeling than the highest respect.'

On 22 January 1852, Zadkiel wrote to Cooke, 'Lord Robert Grosvenor has appointed me to meet him to consult on the matter.' Together with William Ewart, a radical member of Parliament, Grosvenor agreed to try to put Zadkiel's petition, as a private member's bill, to the House of Commons on 16 March. But it apparently fell victim to the Parliamentary timetable, for it failed to appear in the business of that or any succeeding day. And there, for the time being, the matter rested.

Zadkiel's taste for grand schemes had now been whetted. The Great Exhibition took place in 1851, and at Crystal Palace in Hyde Park, three years later removed and reconstructed at Sydenham, Prince Albert led a celebration of industrial and imperial progress. In keeping with the self-confident spirit of this enterprise, Zadkiel conceived a plan for a huge public telescope to be set up on land near Crystal Palace. Under the aegis of the 'Wellington Telescope Company', this project would be the showpiece for a 'British College of Practical Astronomy'. With perceptiveness but extraordinary effrontery, he chose Lord Henry Brougham, the former lord chancellor, as its prospective sponsor. Perceptively, because Brougham was an eminent figure in public life; irascible, brilliant and indefatigable, and as well liked by the public as he was detested by his patrician Whig colleagues, Brougham worked tirelessly on behalf of popular scientific education. But impudently, because the jewel in the crown of his efforts in that respect was probably the violently anti-astrological Society for the Diffusion of Useful Knowledge, which he had founded in 1825. The SDUK merits an explanation, in order to appreciate Zadkiel's true position.

We are already familiar with the attack by Thomas Dick, writing for the SDUK, upon astrologers and John Varley in particular, and with the Society's *British Almanac*, first issued for 1828, which was intended to replace the traditional astrological almanac. It appeared just one year after Raphael's pioneering *Prophetic Messenger*, in a struggle to gain control of roughly the same market. The *Athenaeum* hailed the appearance of the SDUK's new almanac as evidence of its 'resolution to attack ignorance and imposture in one of its strongest holds . . . "The British Almanac" *must* drive the rubbish of the Stationers' Company out of the field. The people *cannot* longer endure to be insulted in their understanding and their moral sense as they have been.' And not only must drive it out, but would. The *London Magazine* of 1828 proclaimed that 'the empire of astrology [is] at an end . . . By the year 1832, (even *we* prophesy) the whole delusion will have vanished before the day-spring of knowledge.'

The prophetic record of astrologers is at least no worse. Writing a few years later, in 1832, Dixon noted:

> I am assured by my bookseller, who has the principal supply of a large district, both manufacturing and agricultural, that notwithstanding all the efforts which have been made to run down 'Moore's Almanack', and introduce the 'British' in its stead, he sells more of the old favourite than ever; if this be the fact generally, which is not at all unlikely, it sufficiently accounts for all the vexation evinced by the 'Diffusion Society's' writers . . . notwithstanding their much vaunted liberality . . . The days for tomahawks and scalping knives are gone by, and 'the Society' should never have suffered itself to be disgraced by avowing a principle of bitter, unqualified, uncalled-for extermination.

It is difficult to dispute Dixon's point and the sales of *Moore's* bear out his bookseller's opinion. Thanks to its over-zealousness, Brougham's SDUK had already fallen well short of its stated goals. Moreover, to add insult to injury, there were also the flourishing new almanacs of Raphael and Zadkiel to contend with. In 1841, Zadkiel mocked the SDUK's scheme to capture the astrological market as a cynical commercial ploy, initiated 'under the Authority of the Society for the Confusion of Useful Knowledge'. His depiction of the *British Almanac's* origins begins:

> Take a 'spirited' publisher; let him gather at his 'hospitable board' a select party of London *savans*. When they have well drunken, let him accidently mention that, although he has lately published some of the most useful works in the world, written by the most talented men imaginable, yet, incomprehensible as it may seem, the sale has been infinitely small, &c. (N.B. The most talented men imaginable are all present) . . .

Indeed, Zadkiel had even analysed Brougham's own nativity in his *The Horoscope* of 1834, commenting unfavourably on his subject's appearance and personality. The latter presented a fairly broad target. His vanity and arrogance, for example, were such that on 8 November 1839, Brougham faked his own death in order to discover the verdict of posterity. A letter from the witness of a fatal carriage accident was received by a friend, who immediately brought it to Gore House, from whence the news quickly spread. The story was believed until Brougham himself, perfectly healthy, appeared the following day, along with his obituary in *The Times*. According to Lord Greville's diary, 'General suspicion immediately fixed itself on Brougham himself, who, finding the bad impression produced, hastened to remove it by a vehement but indirect denial . . . ' Examining the letter, D'Orsay pronounced its handwriting identical with that of the former lord chancellor himself. 'The Duke of Cambridge hunted Brougham round the room, saying: "Oh, by G--, you wrote the letter; by G--, you did it yourself." Brougham is in a state of prodigious excitement.' (Remember, this is the arch-defender of reason and truth.)

Whether or not the episode had suggested the idea to Brougham, an earlier opponent of astrology, Jonathan Swift, had famously faked the death of John Partridge, the leading astrologer of his day. Posing as another astrologer, Swift issued an eyewitness account of Partridge's death-bed confession and the latter's subsequent difficulties in establishing his continued existence became a joke across Europe. No one doubted that of Brougham, however, and some undoubtedly regretted it.

In 1843, through its *Penny Magazine*, the SDUK attacked Raphael and Zadkiel directly, complaining bitterly that

> though there are but a few among the well-informed who believe in judicial astrology, yet there is a rather numerous class with sufficient credulity not only to admit, but to seek its predictions; and, it may be added, that even amongst the better instructed — amongst those who openly denounce every species of divination — there are to be found minds prone to the secret admission of sidereal influence and presages.

Perhaps confirming this suspicion, the austerely earnest *Penny Magazine* went under two years later.

The terms used reveal an upper-middle-class view of astrology as a sort of intellectual and moral plague, with a stigma of quasi-venereal shamefulness. The persistence of this view, and astrology's equally stubborn refusal to disappear, led to a stalemate. In 1851, the *Athenaeum* spluttered, '*Raphael* and *Zadkiel* continue their trade in the credulity of mankind: growing more and more boastful, vulgar, illogical, and mendacious year by year.' And from the opposite perspective, though in equally inflated rhetoric, Zadkiel maintained the same thing. As he wrote in *The Voice of the Stars*, one of his short-lived attempts at a regular astrological publication other than his almanac, astrology 'has been sick, but not dying; silent, but not destroyed. Struck down by foul calumny, fettered by ignorance, slandered by falsehood, pressed to the earth by prejudice; yet lo! it lives, moves, and rises again . . . '

The Wellington Telescope Company — not to mention the British College of Practical Astronomy — was arguably a scheme to advance the cause of astrology under the very noses of its foes. Zadkiel fully appreciated the need for secrecy. On 8 November 1852, he wrote to Cooke:

> As to the matter of your connexion with the Telescope, it strikes me that the best policy will be to have it clearly understood by your friends that it has nothing to do with Astrology, and is merely for the furtherance of the science of Astronomy. The other thing is not yet popular enough to bear naming in the same day with anything to which *public* support may be required.

Cooke was obviously very worried that Brougham might discover Zadkiel's astrological persona. With typically bluff self-confidence, the latter reassured Cooke on 19 November:

> I quite agree in all you mention, except as to Lord B. having any idea *at all* of my being Zadkiel. He no doubt holds Astrology to be such a contemptible affair that he never looked at one of my works, and I would wager hardly knows of their existence . . . I think with you that Lord B. is the man for our purpose, and the *only* man.

Not for the last time, Cooke allowed himself to be persuaded. He wrote to Brougham on 31 December 1852, putting before him the proposal for the telescope. A week later, Brougham replied from his home in Cannes expressing interest. On 5 March 1853, Cooke wrote again with more details; and again on 5 May. But no more replies came, nor to any subsequent enquiries; and two years later, when Cooke arranged to be introduced to Brougham in London, the latter snubbed him outright. As usual, Cooke had been right and Zadkiel wrong: Brougham had almost certainly smelled a rat and made the connection between Cooke, Morrison and Zadkiel. Perhaps pretending more surprise than he felt, Cooke later complained of Brougham: 'His eccentric conduct with reference to the Wellington Telescope Company has never been explained. Nor has there been any explanation of his Lordship's slighting the author when introduced personally to his Lordship by the relative who gave the written introduction in December 1852 . . . '

Brougham had been the key to the plan's success, and without him the rest of the arrangements swiftly unravelled. Aware of his astrological sympathies and value as a public figure, Zadkiel had already approached Bulwer-Lytton. As he wrote to Cooke on 17 December 1852: 'I was with Sir Edward Bulwer-Lytton today for near two hours. Sir Edward will have no objection to our having his name as a Patron, I am sure, if we can first have Lord B.' But in the spring of 1853, the wily author also declined to lend his name to the project, 'not being,' he explained, 'an astronomer'.

This response was entirely in character. Bulwer-Lytton had already refused publicly to support John Elliotson, a Professor of Medicine at University College London, who was obliged to resign in 1838 for his advocacy of mesmerism. He also persistently failed to endorse Daniel D. Home, the leading spiritualist in England in the 1850s and '60s, despite professing enthusiasm and attending many of his seances. Home later complained of Bulwer-Lytton, 'In public he was an investigator of Spiritualism, in private a believer.' And in 1870, he was approached by Hargraves Jennings, the impoverished author of a recent tract on the rites and mysteries of the Rosicrucians, for a reference to help him to obtain a job as a librarian. Bulwer-Lytton refused even this much, offering him instead the cold comfort of congratulations on his 'learning and acuteness'.

Zadkiel was thus brought up short. Unabashed, he turned his attention to more personally lucrative enterprises. Once again, Cooke was duped not only into acting as the legal and public relations representative, but also into doing most of the work. The Glamorgan & Cardiff Coal Company, born on 21 March 1853, struggled through the next four years before being written off. All its backers — except, somehow, Zadkiel himself — lost heavily, including the principal investor, a retired admiral. Cooke himself lost more than £1,000. Through hard work and a measure of luck, he just managed to avoid the same fate for Zadkiel's next brainwave, the Emperor Life Assurance Company; also begun in 1853, it was successfully sold three years later.

Meanwhile Cooke had been working to realize one of his own sober ambitions. In 1854, his first book appeared: *A Plea For Urania*. Despite a very reasonable price, it sold less than 250 copies over the next six years. Eventually, it was quietly remaindered by Cooke's publisher without consultation, a cruel fate for 388 well-written and thorough pages. Cooke's only mistake was to address in measured tones those whose minds were already largely made up, without either the sensationalism that would have attracted a more popular audience, or the technical details needed actually to practise astrology.

In addition to providing an elegant overview of the history and branches of astrology, and of religious and scientific objections against it, Cooke drew upon his own recent experiences. Discussing the legal situation, he noted:

> The simple fact is, that if — in cases of persons apprehended for practising what is *not* fortune-telling but real astrology — evidence in favour of the science should be admitted, the *pretence* and *deception* (which constitute the essence of the supposed crime), would fall to the ground entirely; and so Sidrophel would get off altogether. This would never do; it would not suit the ignorant prejudices of the magistracy, who fear the science without knowing why.

(Sidrophel was the name of the astrologer in *Hudibras*, a seventeenth-century satire.)

The *Plea* received as little critical as popular notice. The *Sun* gave a bemused but friendly reception to this 'wild and 'wildering phantasmagoria', but the *Morning Advertiser* and *Morning Post* were hostile. Cooke therefore paid for various advertisements, one of which promptly appeared in *The York Journal* as 'A Plea for Mania'. The longest notice, and a reasonably serious one, appeared in the *Illustrated London Magazine* for December 1854. Discussing astrology itself, the writer acknowledged, 'This crazy old lady still jogs along the great highway of life', carrying on

> just as she did in the days of the old Roman satirist, and just as she did in Egypt, Chaldea, and the Assyrian plains centuries before. It is true that science, wit, learning, and religion have all inflicted heavy blows and sore discouragements on her; yet, somehow or other, she totters along — nay, not only totters — at times advances with head erect and all the dignity of impudence . . .
>
> The Old Arabian astronomers of the eighth and ninth centuries were forced to recommend the truths of science to the Egyptian courts by appearing in the guise of astrologers: poor old Astrology can only obtain a hearing, in the nineteenth century, by adopting the language of science, and talking big about 'reason', and 'probabilities', and 'astral phenomena', and 'celestial philosophy' . . .
>
> The great death blow, to our minds, to the 'Plea for Urania', is, that she has been pleading for centuries, and has never yet established herself in the good graces of men of science. Napoleon used to say that the only sure mark of a good general is success — this we take to hold equally well of a true science. Tried by this touchstone, Astrology fails.

But astrologers could have replied with W.S. Cross's riposte to the SDUK in 1849: 'Surely if it were nothing better than "the most splendid fiction that has ever been imposed on the credulity of mankind",' its alleged falsehood and absurdity might have been proved and established by its opponents in less than 3,000 years.' Thus the old stalemate, or its intellectual extension, continued unchanged.

This outcome was very unsatisfactory for Cooke, of course. Ten years later, he bitterly recalled Zadkiel's interpretation of a horary map that the former had requested on 30 March 1853, about his *Plea*'s chances of success. Zadkiel had replied, 'The position of the Moon shows some popularity and credit, but much opposition, as truth in this world is always opposed. You shall have my aid with pleasure. RJM.' Cooke did not lose faith in astrology as a consequence of his disillusionment with Zadkiel, however. His own verdict was that 'Zadkiel's "Judgement" as usual was exaggerated and inaccurate . . . The whole figure denotes merely partial success and much loss.'

No one could say Zadkiel himself quit easily, however; and Cooke too remained anxious to advance the cause of astrology where his book and the Wellington Telescope Company had failed. Reluctant to give up entirely on Bulwer-Lytton, Zadkiel persuaded Cooke to write again on 2 March 1860, asking him 'at least' to become the patron of a 'Congress of Astronomers and Friends of Astral Science', with R. J. Morrison as treasurer. But the old author was too wily for that and from his London home in Park Lane, he replied on 13 March 1860: 'Sir — I regret that I cannot offer any assistance to your scheme, which I return. I do not profess to any authority in the science treated of, and I cannot give my name to projects of which I am not competent to form a judgement. Yrs &c., E. Bulwer-Lytton.'

Undeterred, Zadkiel decided to proceed with an Astro-Meteorological Society anyway and Cooke agreed to act as solicitor. The proposal was not, however, received with universal acclaim. Cooke recalled 'it was feared by some of its members that the cloven hoof peeped out on account of the word "Astro" being introduced in the wording of the prospectus of the Society!' None the less, a first meeting took place in Cooke's legal rooms at 58 Pall Mall, on 29 November 1860. Zadkiel revealed its intended purpose in a note to Cooke of 8 January 1861: 'I agree with you that if Astrology is ever to make its way within the public it must be through the means of Astro-Meteorology as an introduction.'

The Society met again in January 1861 and held its first annual general meeting on 29 November 1861. When Zadkiel published a critique of one

Admiral Fitzroy's system in *The Times*, however, the strain became too great. A sizeable minority of members left the Society, 'chiefly,' as Cooke put it, 'because they maintained that it was connected with astrological science, which was an undeniable fact, although some refined attempts were made to prove the contrary'. One member admitted privately to Cooke, 'The scientific man will not consent to hear of Astrology in the present day.' In March 1862, the Society dissolved itself.

Once again, Cooke's hopes had been dashed. 'The permanent establishment of the Astro-Meteorological Society,' he wrote,

> would have been the means of introducing and of popularizing astrological facts, by means of deductive reasoning, in a clear, positive, and satisfactory manner; because it would have been proved that the planets affected the Earth according to their angular positions; and then their influences upon its inhabitants might have been shown in a similar manner, giving a tangible reason for the 'horoscope' ... Astrology would cease to be treated as a superstition, for it would be proved to be 'a scientific art', namely experience reasoned upon and then brought under general principles, as distinguished from merely accumulated experience, which is simply *empiricism*.

Neither Cooke's ambition nor the chosen means, astro-meteorology, were new; they had both been entertained by leading English astrologers, for example, two centuries earlier. In Cooke's view — and again, this was an old idea, although restimulated perhaps by recent discoveries in spectroscopy — the Sun's rays reflected by each planet on to the Earth contain the unique chemical properties of that planet, which 'so excite different phenomena'. However difficult to prove, this enterprise seemed more promising than facing the bald question: How can distant planets indicate the destiny of a child? Astrologers were thus thrown back once more on the reply, to quote Cross again, '*How should I know*? It is found by observation and experience that they do so indicate: and we are not justified in rejecting that fact, because we cannot account for it.' In other words, 'empiricism'.

In 1860 began the most dramatic episode in Zadkiel's life. Unsurprisingly, given the nature of both the man and the subject-matter, it culminated in a public sensation in mid-Victorian society. The tiny stone which triggered the avalanche was a prediction by Zadkiel in his *Almanac for 1861*, published in the autumn of 1860. Discussing the full moon in March 1861, Zadkiel wrote,

> the stationary position of Saturn in the third degree of Virgo in May, following upon this lunation, will be very evil for all persons born on or near the 26th August; among the sufferers I regret to see the worthy Prince Consort of these realms. Let such persons pay scrupulous attention to health.

There matters might have rested, had not Prince Albert apparently obliged 'The Voice of the Stars' by suddenly dying on 14 December 1861. This was a severe shock and had momentous political as well as more personal effects. In addition to his involvement in various projects, of which the Great Exhibition was the most public, Albert in his capacity as prince consort represented to many of his subjects a semi-divine figure, the object of daily prayers across the realm.

This much larger stone promptly dislodged a shower when one Alderman Humphery publicly remarked in court on Zadkiel's apparent accuracy. It is not clear whether Humphery was one of his fans; if so, he was a most unusual judge in that respect. This was too much for that paragon of respectability, the *Daily Telegraph*, and on 31 January 1862 it leapt to the defence of the late prince and what he represented with this editorial:

> We should rejoice to hear that the police had routed out the 'cunning' men who lurk in garrets in poor neighbourhoods, and delude inexperienced girls and frivolous young married women. But, at the same time, we claim an equal need of justice to be applied to an imposter quite as impudent and thrice as mischievous as the beggar, the gypsy, or the 'cunning man'. There is a fellow who calls himself ZADKIEL, and who for thirty-two years, it seems, has been suffered to publish annually a farrago of wretched trash which he calls an almanac, and in which, pretending to interpret the 'voice of the stars', he gives vent to a mass of predictions on public affairs. Once in every five years or so, one of Zadkiel's prophecies, which are generally the

stupidest jumping at probable eventualities, may by an accident come true; whereupon the seer goes into raptures of the 'Right again!' description, and sells his almanac, we are sorry to learn, by thousands. Very recently the public were scandalised to hear that a London alderman, in the very performance of his magisterial functions, had so little respect for the dignity of the Bench as to call the attention of newspaper reporters to one of Zadkiel's predictions for 1861, which had a kind of hazy coincidence with the death of the Prince Consort. The Almanac has gone up prodigiously in the market, we are told, since Alderman HUMPHERY's ill-advised escapade; but it now becomes the duty of the press to apply a corrective to aldermanic folly, and to expose this Zadkiel in his true colours . . . it shall not be our fault if this mischievous deluder is not in the long run morally tarred and feathered, and has not his ears nailed to the pump.

Turning to *Zadkiel's Almanac for 1862*, the *Daily Telegraph* snarled:

We might pass this rubbishing pamphlet by with contempt; but the publicity it has recently attained demands that it and its author, whoever he may be, should be exposed and denounced. The one is a sham, the other is a swindler. The Almanac is no mere harmless catchpenny; its contents are calculated to alarm the timid and to mislead the credulous; and as to the allusion to LORD PALMERSTON, and the speculations on the probable duration of life of that illustrious statesman, we regard them as disgustingly and unspeakably wicked. Who is this Zadkiel, and are there no means of ferreting him out, and hauling him up to Bow Street under the statute as a rogue and a vagabond?

This was not the only shaft aimed at Zadkiel and astrology in 1862. In April, *The Times*, reviewing a book about ancient astronomy, gave thanks that Greek astronomy had 'already been placed on a safe scientific footing' (and the juxtaposition of those two adjectives is not coincidental) before the advent of astrology. This questionable chronology is less important than the rhetoric, for the writer's chief purpose was to describe not the ancient world but contemporary London:

Chaldean adventures began to reap a rich harvest in Rome from the wealthy parvenus and ignorant nobility; but accurate knowledge had reached a point that the permanent interests of the human race were safe; and astrology even when most prevalent was a passion, like table-turning or spirit-rapping in our own time, chiefly of those to whom morbid excitement had become a necessity: silly women, worn-our fashionables, and unprincipled adventurers.

The *London Review* too weighed in, twitting Alderman Humphery and laying bare the dreadful wares of astrologers and the like, enticing a helpless populace:

> ... no wise man will regard with indifference the existence or progress of superstition. The best of us is not so far removed from its allures that he can afford to despise the snares which it lays for the uneducated ... When Sir Bulwer-Lytton writes romances of the Mumbo Jumbo order, no wonder that Zadkiel can persuade the old women that their fate depends on the hour of their birth.

It is worth pausing to note a few things about these literary assaults, beginning with the depth of feeling reflected in the strength and at times violence of their language. As Cooke once noted respecting Zadkiel, 'that there was much *personal* feeling mixed up with the attacks, caused probably by this Seer's free-and-easy remarks upon persons and things in general, was pretty clear, irrespective of the usual fear of "letting in" astrology'. Yet the writers clearly felt themselves to be attacking no mere folly, but rather, however unlikely it may seem to us, a dangerous institution and practice that threatened the moral and intellectual well-being, if not indeed 'the permanent interests of mankind'. Nor is that last noun accidently gendered: women are consistently counted among the helpless and innocent victims of imposture. Along with the unlettered masses, they need the firm male hand of science and religion and cannot really be blamed for occasional lapses without it. No, blame is heaped rather upon the heads of conniving members of the gentry and nobility who have deserted their posts, leaving only a handful of middle-class and male defenders of reason, virtue and industry to guard the pass.

Oddly enough, Zadkiel felt at least equally beleaguered, although arguably with more reason, by some similar demons. In his almanac for the following year, he warned in characteristically melodramatic fashion:

> It is, indeed, too true, that astrology, and all its spiritual influence on the human heart, have been rejected; and, instead thereof, infidelity in religion, want of faith in the goodness of God, scientific atheism, have appeared. These have brought in their train the demons of crime, grovelling vice, all the horrors of brutal ignorance, and the retrograde march of civilization. Among the poor we see want and misery, indifference to all true religion ... Among the rich, bloated wealth, sinful and soul-enslaving luxury, cruelty and oppression ... THESE, THESE ARE THE DIRE EVILS REAPED FROM THE MODERN ATTEMPTS TO DECRY THE SCIENCE OF ASTROLOGY.

Zadkiel was perfectly sincere about this. A point of difference between him and Cooke had been the latter's admiration for the pioneering socialism of Robert Owen and his co-operative communities. As Cooke put it with his usual restraint, Zadkiel 'had considerable antipathy to Mr Owen', alluding to 'his "wretched atheism"'. In 1841, Zadkiel even published an essay entitled 'Astrology Overthrows Socialism'. In a seamless blend of genteel piety, social conservatism and astrological principles, he argued that Owen's emphasis on 'the social medium' was mistaken, since 'we may absolutely prove by astrological experience that men are *born* with various mental predispositions or propensities'.

It was one thing to attack socialists, however, and quite another to take on his own powerful antagonists. To a degree, Zadkiel was obviously his own worst enemy, toying with martyrdom when he was already an easy target. But, at this point, the *Daily Telegraph* writer's question as to Zadkiel's identity was not rhetorical; he really did not know the answer.

It was not long in coming. A few days later, this rather wonderful letter appeared in the issue of 1 February:

Sir — In your impression of this day you ask who is this Zadkiel, and are there no means of ferreting him out and handing him up to Bow Street under the statute as a rogue and vagabond. I will aid you on the scent by first informing you that he stands as a lieutenant on the Navy List, seniority 1815. Next, that he has his admirers about Greenwich Hospital, who fancy him a prophet A1, and that his mischievous propensities are not solely involved in that foolish publication 'Zadkiel's Almanac'. More, I think he gave his name not long since as president of some peculiar society connected with astrology (R. J. Morrison). A friend reminds me that the author of 'Zadkiel' is the celebrated crystal globe seer, who gulled many of our nobility about the year 1852, making use of a boy under fourteen or a girl under twelve; he pretended, by their looking into the crystal globe, to hold converse with the spirits of the Apostles, even our Saviour, with all the angels of light as well as darkness, and to tell what was going on in any part of the world. Drawings were made of the objects seen in these visions. One noble lady gave one of these boys £5 to communicate intelligence respecting her son, who was in the Mediterranean. That boy peached — let the cat out of the bag. Of course the information was false. The seer took the money — if he really be the same — for these profane acts, and made a good thing of it. If it be deemed sufficiently important, there can be no doubt that he could be satisfactorily ferreted out. As to his position as a naval officer, excepting in the coastguard, he has not served afloat since 1815. —
I am, Sir, Yrs., &c.,   ANTI-HUMBUG

Zadkiel immediately engaged a solicitor and instructed him to ascertain the identity of Anti-humbug. Eventually, the *Daily Telegraph* succumbed to pressure and revealed him to be an archetypal resident of the Home Counties, who might have been invented if he had not really existed, namely Rear-Admiral Sir Edward Belcher. Belcher's naval experience was mainly in exploring and surveying in the Pacific and the Bering Strait. In 1852, he had been placed in charge of an unsuccessful expedition to find Sir John Franklin in the Arctic north-west; the *Dictionary of National Biography* records dispassionately that among those serving with and under him, 'Perhaps no officer of equal ability has ever succeeded in inspiring so much dislike.'

Meanwhile, Cooke had rushed into print with a booklet entitled *Astrology in a Nut-Shell. A Letter to Mr Alderman Humphery.* In it, he again pointed out the anomaly of hundreds of thousands of astrological readers, if not believers, coexisting with their criminalization by Section 4 of the Vagrancy Act. In an aside pointing to his own increasing disillusionment, he added,

> My experience has informed me that the chief objection [to astrologers] consists in the uncongenial character of the doctrines, when considered with respect to the habits and customs of this age. For this reason, I should hesitate to recommend any person to become entangled in their meshes even as an amateur, unless prepared for social ostracism, and the life of a literary Robinson Crusoe.

As usual, however, Cooke's quiet voice was drowned in the babel of passionate intensity.

Upon learning Belcher's identity, Zadkiel demanded a public apology and retraction of the obvious slander. The former refused, so Zadkiel initiated a libel suit. Twice delayed at Belcher's request, the trial was finally ordered to be heard at the Court of Queen's Bench on 29 June 1863. Before proceeding to the trial, however, what were these crystal-gazing sessions before a 'gulled' nobility to which Belcher had referred?

Here we must return briefly to Lady Blessington's house at Kensington Gore — the site of similar sessions in the 1840s, led by Varley, with Bulwer-Lytton and Disraeli in attendance. The contents of Gore House were auctioned off to pay her debts after her flight to Paris in 1849. Among the objects sold was the centrepiece on those occasions, a large crystal ball given to Lady Blessington by her friend Nazim Pasha. Although it is possible that Zadkiel himself was at the auction, more probably the ball was purchased by an astute antiques dealer from Brompton, west London, who sold it to him shortly afterwards.

The dealer might have known that Zadkiel would be unable to resist it. Scrying, or divination by means of a crystal, was already a venerable part of occult tradition when the sixteenth-century magus John Dee took it up, aided by a louche young man named Edward Kelley, who acted as Dee's scryer. The result was many manuscript pages of conversations with angels and archangels, obliging Dee's unslakable thirst for knowledge of the secrets of the universe.

Nor had scrying disappeared from nineteenth-century England. Francis Barrett discussed it and supplied instructions in his book *The Magus*. Frederick Hockley was a spiritualist Freemason, and accountant by day, who once worked for Barrett's occult colleague, the bookseller John Denley. By the 1870s, Hockley had amassed more than thirty manuscript volumes of such questions and answers. And in the 1850s, Christopher Cooke corresponded for a while with J. G. H. Brown, a spiritualist crystal-gazer with a few hundred followers in and around Nottingham, whose main informant was the angel Gabriel. Brown published *A Message from the World of Spirits* in 1857. Eventually, Cooke wrote:

> I discovered so much incongruity and uncertainty with respect to certain predictive statements which were made, that, notwithstanding the beauty, harmony, and ingenuity of the system of spiritual life promulgated, I was compelled to discard the statements entirely, not knowing what parts to believe, nor what parts to disbelieve, with safety, taken by themselves. This I much regretted.

All this Zadkiel well knew, and without the benefit of Cooke's finer scruples. It also fitted well with Zadkiel's magico-spiritual conception of astrology:

> None of the great men who have taught and practised astrology have ever supposed that the brute masses of planetary bodies could influence the minds of mortals. They ever held that those bodies were the habitations of good and evil angels; and that it was by *their* actions that mundane events were operated.

Also, crystals were customarily consecrated to particular planets, which implied certain days of the week and hours of the day when they could best be used. Zadkiel believed that his was ruled by Michael, the angel of the Sun. Later, he acquired a guardian angel named Hartiel, whose revelations, as he wrote to a friend, 'are very wonderful, and very interesting and instructive. He will not appear in Lady Blessington's crystal, as "aerial" and evil spirits have been and are in it. But he appears in Mr Brown's crystal, and in the new one I have.'

The ability to scry was uncommon and thought of by its proponents in much the same way as 'psychic abilities' are considered today by theirs: i.e. a property of the unusually gifted and of children before they are taught otherwise. Such gifts ought to be discernible in the person's nativity, and Zadkiel speculated with Cooke as to the appropriate configuration: an angular Venus, he thought, and perhaps a strong ninth house. (The ninth house in a nativity signifies that person's religious tendencies and abilities. It is obvious why such a pragmatic attitude to the sacred had long failed to find favour with the church.)

Zadkiel immediately began experimenting and had his first vision in the crystal on 29 January 1850. Whether this was a personal experience, which he denied, or second-hand through one of his children, who often acted as his scryers, is not clear. In either case, he could not contain his excitement and a series of private sessions with the crystal began, which lasted until February of the next year. Showing his usual recklessness, he even wrote about them, as Morrison, to the *Athenaeum*.

Although, or perhaps because, the *Athenaeum* published a scathing mention of these sessions, concluding that 'The Impostor of our day does not seek the hovel for his Fool', word soon spread. Interest was partly stimulated by early visions in the crystal of Arctic scenes. This was in the context of intense public interest in the fate, as yet unknown, of Sir John Franklin and his ships, which had set out in 1845 to discover the North-West Passage. Lady Franklin sent for Morrison and soon the crystal featured in high society gatherings throughout London. It seems there was a new appetite in high society for metaphysical exotica, beyond the perennial search for titillation and personal reassurance. Cooke was frequently present at these sessions. Reflecting one of his own central preoccupations, he once asked, 'Is astrology lawful?' The answer returned, 'Is God ashamed of His own works?'

Such were the episodes to which Belcher was referring in his letter and any of the nobility reading it, who had been present, might have shifted uneasily at this rather public airing of their unorthodoxy. Zadkiel had already given detailed accounts of the visions on some of these occasions in his 1851 and 1852 *Almanac*. The revelations bolstered his subsequent circulation figures, but they probably escaped the attention of most regular readers of the quality newspapers. Those readers were about to be treated to a feast, however.

The case of *Morrison vs. Belcher, Knight* took place on 29 June 1863 before a special jury. Sir Alexander Cockburn, the lord chief justice, presided. Mr Serjeant Shee acted for Morrison, the plaintiff, and Mr Serjeant Ballantine for the defendant Belcher. The latter pleaded 'Not guilty', asserting that the alleged libels were true in substance and fact, but he offered no witnesses in his defence. As the *Morning Advertiser* reported the next day, 'The court was crowded, and among the auditory were numerous distinguished persons, nobility and gentry, who had their nativities cast and their fortunes told by aid of the horoscope, the particular planet under which they were born, and "the voice of the stars".' *The Times* too, which also carried a full report, allowed that 'This was a case of a very extraordinary character.'

Mr Shee, opening the case for Zadkiel, said that the plaintiff was a lieutenant in the Royal Navy and, having distinguished himself in that profession, had retired from the service and become a student of astronomy and, among other things, astrology. He was also the editor and proprietor of *Zadkiel's Almanac*, which had obtained an enormous circulation and great notoriety in consequence of his having predicted the death of the prince consort. Alderman Humphery having made some particular observations upon the statements in *Zadkiel's Almanac*, the circumstance was commented on in a leading article in one of the daily papers. Afterwards, a letter signed 'Anti-humbug', which was of a most scurrilous nature, appeared in the same journal and he would be able to prove that the writer of it was the defendant.

The letter, after making some very severe comments, went on to answer the enquiry as to 'Who is this Zadkiel?' It mentioned the name of R.J. Morrison, who was also identified as the celebrated crystal seer. Here Mr Shee alluded learnedly to John Aubrey's *Miscellanies*, where mention is made of 'a consecrated beryl', a kind of crystal. The defendant's letter went on to say the services of a boy had been engaged, but the boy had 'peached' and thus the whole affair had been exposed. This, then, was the substance of his client's complaint: that he was called in effect a wilful impostor. Mr Shee hoped that the jury would not be diverted from the real question to such mysteries as that of animal magnetism or mesmerism, which had engaged a great deal of attention a few years ago.

Now his client, Mr Morrison, had never for one moment pretended that he had seen visions such as were described, but his son having seen something which he said was connected with the Arctic expedition, Lady Franklin had desired the crystal might be brought to her, and from the publicity given to the scene seen by young Morrison it became quite the rage in the fashionable world. Peers, bishops, ladies of the highest position — all were anxious to see the crystal. So great became the pressure upon Mr Morrison that he was compelled to leave town, and he, Mr Shee, would be able to produce letters written by persons of the highest position written to Mr Morrison, all asking for a view of the crystal. Although an attempt might be made to draw the attention of the jury from the point before them — an action for the recovery of damages for a malicious libel — he felt satisfied that, since Sir Edward had refused to make the apology his client required, they would give his client such damages as would prove he was not the unprincipled impostor the defendant said he was.

Zadkiel was then called to the stand. He made an imposing figure, over six feet tall and stoutly built, dressed in civilian clothes, but with a couple of naval medals pinned to his chest — and the gallery strained to see this modern magus in the flesh. Speaking with dignity, he stated that he was a commander in the Royal Navy. He had since devoted himself a great deal to scientific pursuits and had studied astronomy. After his retirement from the Navy, he had also begun to study the old astrology and had succeeded in correcting the errors, he said, of William Lilly. He had published several works of that nature and was also the proprietor of *Zadkiel's Almanac*. It contained predictions founded upon astronomical contingencies, which he had found mostly true after forty years' experience. In 1861, there was in his almanac a peculiar prediction relative to the death of the prince consort.

At this point, at the request of Mr Ballantine, a copy of the almanac was produced and the passage containing the prediction read from it, plus this other: 'The lunation at the end of November, 1860, gives warning of some suffering near at hand, but let us hope it will not be violent; 1861 is evil for the father of the nation.' Mr Ballantine also quoted Zadkiel's speculations concerning Lords Derby, Cardigan and Palmerston, as well as the evidently imminent death of Lord Brougham. Passages from the almanac for 1851 were added to the record, such as that for a crystal-gazing session on 4 February 1850: 'Judas Iscariot also appears. Is very wretched; did sell Jesus Christ; is in Hell. Asks to be let go from the Crystal.'

Examination of Zadkiel continued. He went on to say that, after Alderman Humphery's comments upon the prediction, he had become aware of the publication of the letter signed Anti-humbug. He had read about crystals and seen them and, hearing that Lady Blessington had had a curious crystal ball, he bought it in 1849 from a dealer in curiosities in Brompton.

Here the crystal ball was produced and, amid barely suppressed merriment, it was handed around the court for examination. It appeared to be a ball of Brazilian rock crystal, about four and a half inches in diameter. Mr Ballantine remarked, 'Some of my younger brethren, gentlemen, are looking into it to see their prospects of future business.' (Great laughter at this.)

Zadkiel went on to say that, when he had set it upon the table before his young son, the latter immediately saw visions relating to the expedition of Sir John Franklin. A young gentleman named Ussher also looked into the ball and saw various things in it which he described. (Ussher was a grandson of the eminent Admiral Sir Thomas Ussher; he soon got into considerable trouble for his involvement and denied his earlier statements about what he had seen.) For himself, Zadkiel said, he never saw anything in it. However, in consequence of what had been announced, various persons of distinction had asked to see it; he held their letters in his hand. Several names were mentioned here, whereupon Mr Ballantine observed that he did not suppose these persons would like their names to be known. Mr Shee replied that he did not at all desire that either, but simply to have the fact noted that they had asked to be allowed to see the ball and that it had only been shown at their request.

Zadkiel said that he had requested several of those persons to attend the trial and he believed they were present. He had never received any money for exhibiting the ball, nor had he ever suggested to the boy or the young man that they should say anything. Moreover, it was untrue that £5 had been given to the boy to say he saw anything in the ball. He had freely lent the crystal to friends, he said, and lent it more often than he had remained with it. Once a servant girl looked at it and said she saw something remarkable: a brother of her master lying ill in a foreign country. From what he had heard, he believed that it had turned out to be the fact. Here the lord chief justice interposed, 'We must not have that. Mere hearsay.'

Zadkiel went on to explain that he had met Sir Edward Belcher at an evening party at Colonel and Mrs Merton's, when the ball was exhibited there, and he had certainly seen nothing to excite disgust, nor did he intimate at the time that he had done so. On the contrary, Sir Edward had shown no aversion to him and had introduced him to Lord and Lady Lonsdale. He himself had never claimed to have seen visions in the globe, but young persons did, and that quite openly. Among others present when this occurred were the late Prussian minister Baron Bunsen, Admiral Fitzclarence, Baron Brunnow, the Countess of Erroll, the Marchioness of Aylesbury, the Bishop of Lichfield, Colonel Phipps, the Honourable Mr Cowper, M.P. and a great many other persons of distinction who had come to look at the crystal. At one time, he said, there were as many as eight ladies of distinction in this house at once, in addition a bishop and an archdeacon, and various members of Parliament. Finally, he produced some drawings made by the young man Ussher of the visions he saw. He solemnly believed that Ussher had seen them, as it was impossible that he could have imagined the things he described.

Following this representation, Zadkiel was cross-examined by Mr Ballantine, beginning with the drawings which had been published in *Zadkiel's Almanac*. His questioning, combined with the replies it drew, caused considerable merriment in the court, which the lord chief justice made no attempt to quash. 'I see Zadkiel looks like a Knight Templar,' he began. (Laughter.)

> — So he is said to have appeared.
> — Then there is Eve, as she seems to have appeared to someone. Perhaps as if she had suddenly been taken ill?
> — A spirit, who called herself Eve. The spirits were always respectably dressed. [Laughter.] They had all the drapery displayed in the drawings.
> — Called herself! Do you think she told an untruth? I hope these spirits are not guilty of false pretences! [Much laughter.]
> — She represented herself as Eve.

Here the lord chief justice interjected, 'Did they communicate by word of mouth? I thought it was all by way of vision.'

'They appeared with legends, as coming out of their mouths.' (Laughter.)

'Then,' Mr Ballantine continued, 'I see Titania, as she appeared in a chariot, and St Luke, as he appeared on several occasions.'

> — The lady you now direct my attention to is Queen Mab, as she appeared in her car drawn by gnats. [Laughter.] The male is a representation of St

Luke.

[Mr Ballantine] You vouch these matters as true? You don't represent them as jokes, but quite seriously, as if you believed it all?

— I don't believe all that Ussher has said . . .

[The lord chief justice] You don't believe what Ussher has said?

— No, my lord, because he has since said that some of the things he disclosed were false. But I believe he saw Eve.

[Mr Ballantine] Pray how did you ascertain who they were? What language did they speak? Our mother Eve is not usually supposed to have understood English. [Laughter.]

— They spoke various languages.

— What language did Eve use?

— English, I believe. [Much laughter.]

— And Orion, what language did he use?

— English.

— And Titania?

— I think English also.

— And above all, St Luke. What language did he speak? You see this would be a question of great interest, for there is a controversy as to what language he wrote in.

— They all spoke in English. [Great laughter, Zadkiel growing increasingly discomfited.] I still say I have persons who see visions in the crystal ball. A vision of the Lord's Supper has appeared in it, and some of the miracles of our Saviour, the feeding of the multitude with five loaves and two fishes, and our Saviour walking upon the water, and two or three of the Apostles.

— What other languages were used?

— Turkish, French, Latin and Hebrew.

— And pray, who interpreted?

— Nobody did. [Laughter].

— These are the sort of things you vouch in your almanac! And you still represent that you have seers who beheld things in this crystal ball? You have had some wonderful visions lately! You think, I suppose, it will benefit your almanac?

— I never thought of profiting from it.

— You prophesy sometimes, I believe?

— No, I never prophesy, I only predict. [Great laughter.] None can prophesy but those who have the spirit of God, and that I don't presume to have. [It is obvious , from the way Zadkiel is obliged to shift his ground between science and religion and back to science again, that he did so as one or the other offered temporarily better refuge.]

— Well, the stars took you in a bit last year. You predicted Lord Brougham's death, did you not?

— I never predict death to anyone; only danger. [Laughter.]

— Oh, he was 'in danger'. But if he had happened to die, you would have taken credit for it! [Laughter.]

— It is an annual prediction; it extends from birthday to birthday. He is in danger until his next birthday.

— Oh, I see. He is 'in danger' until his death; and then he is out of danger. [More laughter.] Then as to Lord Palmerston, pray, is the 'danger' to which you allude from political combinations, or from his health?

— His health. And the public can believe it or not, as they feel disposed. I have made some predictions about Lord Palmerston, but without perfect data I cannot give perfect predictions.

Mr Ballantine went on to ask more questions in the same vein until the lord chief justice interjected, 'Oh really, we have had enough of this.' Mr Ballantine agreed and proceeded to ask Zadkiel whether he answered the questions of persons as to their 'nativities' and whether he received money for this service. The court learned that he advertised in the almanac, that advice could be given to those who were uneasy in their minds and that the 'aspects of the stars' would be taught at £1 a head.

This was advertised under the name of Samuel Smith, who lived, the plaintiff said, in Goswell Street. But his address for correspondence, given in the almanac, was at Brompton, where he also received letters for the sale of Zadkiel's books.

[The lord chief justice] Then, when Samuel Smith receives applications

from persons whose minds are distressed, do you answer the letters?
— Yes, sometimes.

[Mr Ballantine, proceeding] Do you mean to say that you have not made 'calculations' for wealthy persons as late as 1862?
— Yes, I have; a few.
— And received money through Samuel Smith?
— Yes. I have also given instructions in astrology to some persons, but never to very young people.
— This crystal ball – you purchased it in Brompton?
— Yes. I believe it belonged to the celebrated Dr Dee. I was told so, though I have no means of knowing for certain.
— Who was the young seer who had the conversation with Judas Iscariot?
— My son, I believe.
— And Judas Iscariot preferred getting back to a certain place rather than remaining with you in the globe? [Loud laughter.]

The evidence of the plaintiff's son, taken in America, was then read aloud. He testified that he had indeed seen the visions in the globe as described, and that he had never received £5 from a lady for telling her news of her son, who was then in the Mediterranean.

An impressive array of persons of rank, who had happened in private society to have seen the crystal ball, was next called to the stand. Most were ladies; Mr Ballantine asked them no questions, but suggested with some heat that it might have been better had gentlemen been called by the prosecution.

The first witness was Lady Harry Vane. 'The letter put into my hand,' she said,

> is one I wrote relative to seeing the crystal. It was in consequence of something I had heard from my father, the late Earl Stanhope. I went with two friends, but met others there. I saw the ball; a little boy looked into it. He said he saw a great many things, but I cannot recollect how many. Neither I nor my friends paid anything to Lieutenant Morrison.

Responding to questions from Mr Shee, she added, 'Lord Effingham was of the party. It was at Mr Morrison's own house that the exhibition took place.'

The Master of the Temple, the Reverend Mr Robinson, said, 'I saw the crystal twice, once at my own house, and once at Sir John Cockburn's.' (The brother, that is, of the lord chief justice!)

The Bishop of Lichfield firmly stated, 'I was present at my son-in-law's house when the ball was to be exhibited, and I saw it. I have not the least reason in the world to believe that money was paid for the exhibition.'

Lady Egerton of Tatton affirmed:

> The letter in question was written by me. I went to see the crystal ball; some gentlemen too were of the party.
> — And what transpired there?
> — A boy looked into the ball. When I asked him how many guardian angels I had, he said, 'Seven'. [Laughter.] I said that was a rather large number [more laughter], but the boy said most persons had four. I was most courteously received, and I never paid any money for seeing the ball.
> [The Marchioness of Aylesbury] I saw the crystal ball at Mrs Merton's. Several persons were present.
> — Did you make any enquiries?
> — Oh no, I thought it such nonsense. I do not attend voluntarily today; I was subpoenaed. [Much laughter. The Marchioness's reply obviously took Mr Shee aback somewhat.]

The Reverend George Stokes, the plaintiff's ex-father-in-law, said, 'I know the boy Ussher, and the son of Mr Morrison; they were both pupils of mine. Mr Morrison's wife was my daughter. I thought Mr Morrison was deceived as to what he thought about the ball, but he professed that young persons saw visions in the ball, and I am certain that he believed they did.'

Mr Fulham Webster, a director of the New River Company residing in Berkshire recalled:

> The first time I went was with a lady, and the second time Mr Reynolds was with me. I was not so happy as to receive a great quantity of guardian

angels.

— Can you recall any of the questions put to the seer?

— I believe one of the questions asked was where Swedenborg is now to be found.

Another distinguished witness was the Earl of Wilton, the older brother of Zadkiel's advocate in Parliament, Baron Ebury. Like the others, he said, he had merely seen this ball in society; in his case, at Colonel Merton's. Mr Ballantine playfully asked him whether he had derived any information or advice from it which had been of any particular service to him (laughter), to which the earl replied in the negative. 'Pray,' repeated Mr Ballantine, playing to the gallery, 'did you see any particular "conjunction" it suggested to you, any sort of "combination"?' The earl laughed, and said no.

The next witness testified:

> I am the widow of Colonel Merton. I requested Mr Morrison to bring the crystal ball to my house. On the first occasion, it was shown to friends of mine. There was a large party of us. A young lady and gentleman looked into the ball, and were asked questions as to what they saw. The ball was brought to my house five or six times.
>
> — Was Sir Edward Belcher present?
>
> — He was present on two or three occasions. I even recollect him asking me to get Mr Morrison to bring the ball. It was brought and examined by his friends. Sir Edward did not ask any questions about it.
>
> — Was any money exchanged?
>
> — Nothing was paid, nor was any money given for the ball being brought. It was an evening party . . .

The lord chief justice interrupted: 'The ball was brought for amusement, then, and not for the purpose of prying into secrets of the past?'

'No, purely for scientific amusement.' (Laughter.)

The following witness testified: 'I am the wife of Captain Hoseason, of the Royal Navy. I first saw the crystal ball at "High Beach". I was intimately acquainted with young Ussher.' Upon Mr Shee asking her, 'Had you any reason to suppose the boy was trying to deceive you?' he again received an unexpected answer: 'Yes, I thought he was.'

Then Mr Charles Kent took the stand, stating:

> I am a member of the bar, and the proprietor and editor of the *Sun* newspaper. I know the plaintiff very well. I recollect seeing the crystal ball several years ago. It was at No. 1, Park Lane that the ball was exhibited. There were altogether four persons present, amongst whom was Sir Edward Bulwer-Lytton. A servant looked into the ball, and after gazing at it for some time, she said she saw a man apparently either dying or dead, with his eyes closed and lying down. She said she saw a very curious tree, and described a house with a number of turrets. It appeared to me to resemble Knebworth Park, with which the girl's description corresponded. The girl had never been there. I gave no money, and heard no mention of any being given.
> — Whose was the residence in Park Lane, and who was present?
> — It is Sir Edward Lytton's. Lieutenant Morrison, Sir Edward, myself, and a domestic servant were present. It was the servant who described Sir Edward's country house.
> — Although she had never been there?
> — Yes.

Cross-examining, Mr Ballantine asked Mr Kent to say whose property at Knebworth Park had been described. Upon receiving the reply that it was Sir Edward Lytton's, he remarked scornfully, 'Oh, she described her own master's country seat, did she?'

Sir Edward Bulwer-Lytton himself was then called (not something he would have relished). 'I recollect seeing the ball exhibited at my house,' he agreed.

> It was seen by a domestic servant, whom I had engaged abroad as a cook. She looked in the glass, and described a place like my house in the

country, but she might have seen pictures of it. I do not think anything remarkable occurred afterwards, or I should certainly have made a note of it.

— How did you come to meet Mr Morrison?

— He was introduced to me by a gentleman of very high attainments and the highest honour, a great friend of mine, Mr Kent. No money was paid for the exhibition of the ball, most certainly.

The penultimate witness for the prosecution was an elderly lady, Mrs Allen. She was unshakeable in her account.

I looked at the ball on one occasion. I first saw the reflection of my mother, who has been dead fifty years, with a child in her arms. The ball then became cloudy, and upon clearing both figures had disappeared. Then I saw a man clad in full armour, with a brass helmet on his head, and a lady in a pink dress who leaned on his shoulder. [Laughter.] It was altogether a scene of the most singular and mysterious nature. I shall never forget it as long as I live.

At this obviously sincere testimony, there was perhaps a passing moment — the first — of general discomfort in the court.

Mr Ballantine, cross-examining, was quick to release any such tension:

Are you quite sure of what you saw?

— There could be no mistake about what I saw.

— Did Mr Morrison tell you who the man in armour was?

— He said it was the presiding spirit of the crystal. [Laughter.]

— Did you learn the names of the two persons who were in such loving converse together?

— I did not, nor have I seen either of them since. [More laughter.]

— Pray, are you one of the mediums he advertises?

— No Sir, I have not that honour. [Yet more laughter.]

— You have a firm belief in it, Madam? You have always seen something in it, whenever you looked at it?

— Yes.

Above: A portrait of John Varley by William Blake.

Above: William Blake and John Varley arguing (a sketch by John Linnell).

Opposite: John Varley's nativity of Hannah Palmer.

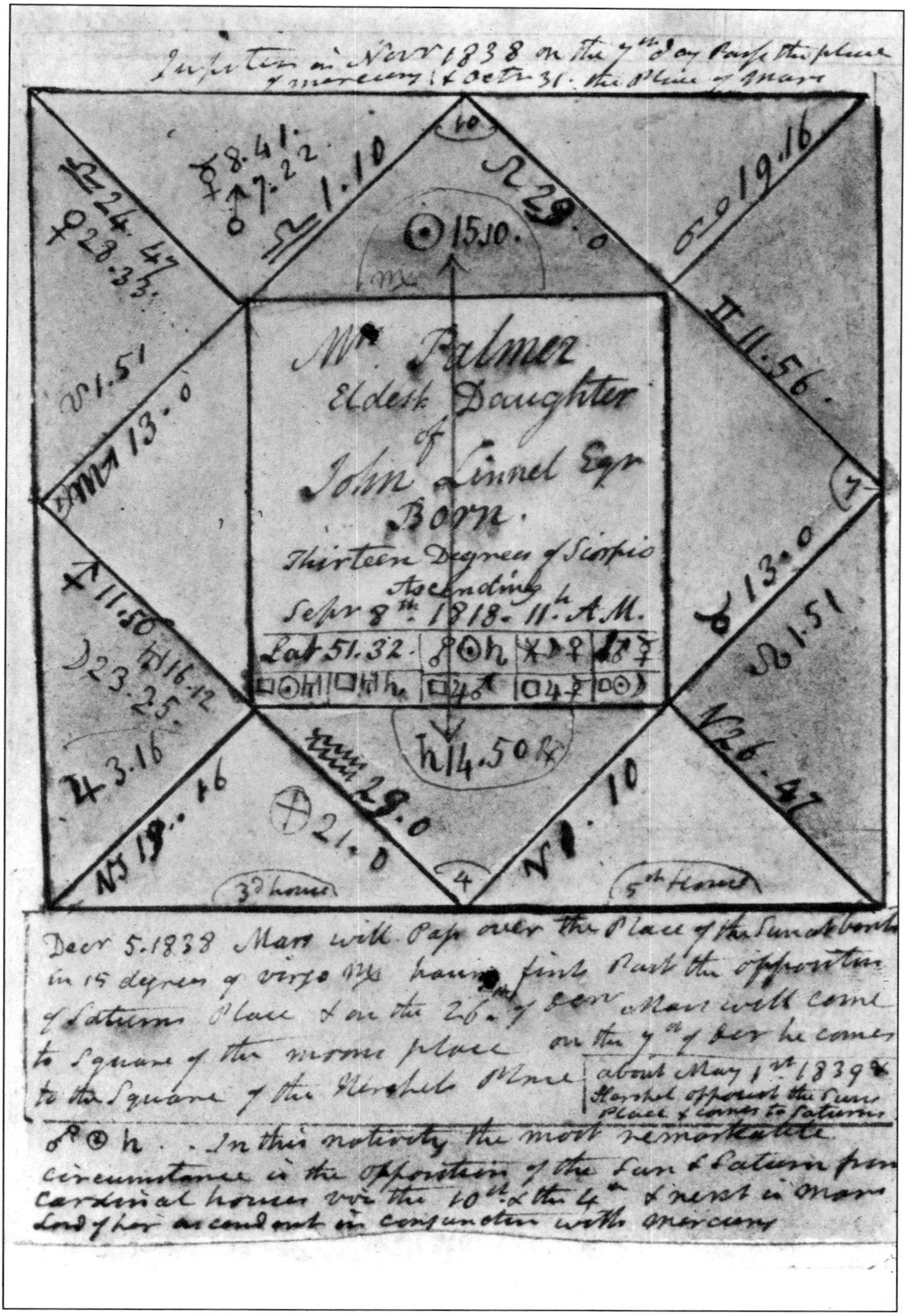

Jupiter in Novr 1838 on the 7th day passes the place of mercury & Octr 31. the place of Mars

Mr Palmer
Eldest Daughter
of
John Linnel Esqr
Born.
Thirteen Degrees of Scorpio
Ascending
Sepr 8th 1818. 11h A.M.
Lat 51.32

☉ 15.10

♄ 14.50 ℞

⊕ 21.0

Decr 5. 1838 Mars will pass over the place of the Sun about both in 15 degrees of virgo ♍ having first past the opposition of Saturns place & on the 26 of Decr Mars will come to square of the moons place on the 9th of Decr he comes to the Square of the Herschel place about May 1st 1839 ☿ Herschel opposed the Suns place & comes to Saturns

☍ ☉ ♄ . In this nativity the most remarkable circumstance is the opposition of the Sun & Saturn from cardinal houses viz the 10th & the 4th & next is Mars lord of her ascendant in conjunction with mercury

Above: Bulwer-Lytton in his study at Knebworth House (a painting by E.M. Ward).

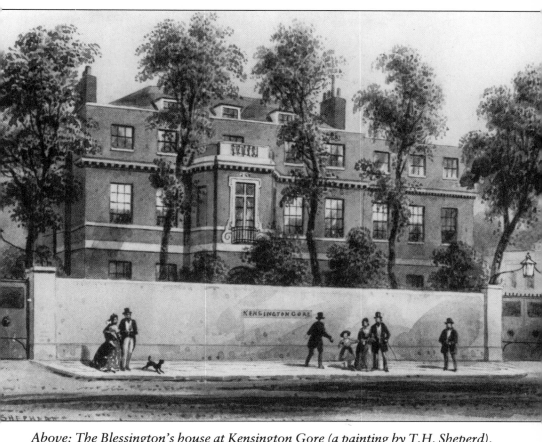

Above: The Blessington's house at Kensington Gore (a painting by T.H. Sheperd).

A MANUAL OF ASTROLOGY,

or the

Book of the Stars.

BEING THE ART OF FORETELLING FUTURE EVENTS.

By the influences of the

Heavenly Bodies

In a manner unattempted by any former Author and divested of the Superstitions of the Dark Ages.

By Raphael.

"The Author of the Astrologer of the Nineteenth Century."
"The Prophetic Messenger," &c. &c.

"The Book of past Times shall be unsealed"

Ancient Prophecy

LONDON:

C. S. ARNOLD,

Tavistock Street, Covent Garden.

MDCCCXXVIII.

Above: A hieroglyphic from Raphael's Prophetic Messenger.

Opposite: The title-page of Raphael's Manual of Astrology.

Above: Zadkiel, aged seventy-six.

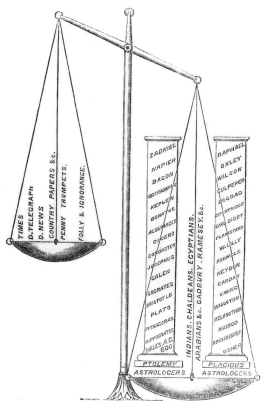

Above: The Scales of Justice, from Zadkiel's Almanac for 1870.

Above: Alan Leo's gold pen and seal (the caduceus of Mercury and the symbol for Uranus).

Above: A.J. Pearce.

Above: The Queen of the Fairies, as she appeared in Zadkiel's crystal.

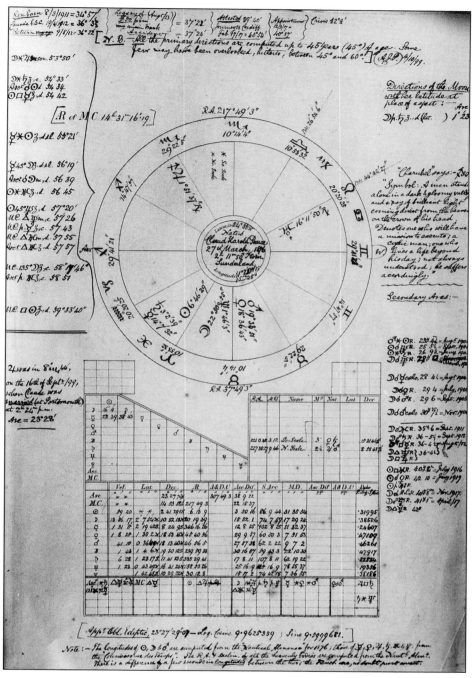

Above: A nativity calculated and drawn up by A.J. Pearce.

Above: Richard Garnett.

Above: Alan Leo's portrait and nativity.

Above: A front-cover of Modern Astrology.

Above: Sepharial.

Above: Alan and Bessie Leo on holiday in Cannes.

— You probably are sure you would see something in it again?

And here Mr Ballantine produced the ball, which he asked the witness to look into. But with much indignation she replied, 'I refuse to look on the crystal in court. It is too solemn a thing to be laughed at, Sir.' (Roars of laughter.)

'Oh Madam! If you look at it in that light, I won't ask you.' And amid gales of amusement, the witness withdrew.

Finally, a young woman, Miss Mary White, was called. She gave somewhat similar evidence, only her experience appeared to have been principally of landscape. 'I have on two occasions seen scenes in the crystal,' she said firmly. 'On the first occasion I saw a Swiss scene, with the snow falling, and on the other a ruined abbey.'

This closed the case for the plaintiff and Mr Ballantine announced that he would call no witnesses.

Mr Shee then addressed the jury on behalf of Zadkiel. He said that he saw the case for the defence would, as he had anticipated, consist of ridiculing the plaintiff's astrology. But that was beside the issue, which was whether he had been guilty of wilful imposture for the purpose of financial advantage. The jury could not be certain that these people, under the influence of excited fancy, did not think they saw what they said they saw; and, in any case, could they really find that the plaintiff had wilfully deluded the gentry and nobility of this country in order to make money? It was also notable that although Sir Edward Belcher had had the spirit to write an anonymous libel, he had not the courage to get into the witness box and attempt to prove the truth of his assertion. In short, the defendant had altogether failed to show that Commander Morrison was the gross imposter he had said he was and, that being the case, it became their duty to find in his favour.

Mr Ballantine now addressed the jury on behalf of Sir Edward, a gentleman, he said, of world-wide fame, whose name was well known in connection with many adventurous expeditions. He was by no means disposed to treat this case merely as one for ridicule. He rather felt disposed to denounce with indignation a scandalous trick and imposture. As to evidence, all evidence would be worthless unless the jury were already convinced (as he hoped they were) that this was an imposture and were anxious to put an end by their verdict to a system of super-stition fostered by foolish women and some men who were worse. One would have thought that in the nineteenth century we had got above and beyond such delusions; but unhappily, day by day it was made manifest that we were not. There had been conjurers and imposters in every age and they were also to be found in our own. These were the old tricks which had imposed upon people in every age. The very works which his learned friend had referred to showed it; and, as a matter of public discussion and free comment, his client and anyone else had a right to brand them as impostures, and profitable impostures. If they were not so, then fortune-telling too was not unlawful, and many an old gypsy was trotting away on the treadmill because she could not have the benefit of his learned friend's lucid exposition of her particular imposture. (Much laughter.)

What did it matter, he continued, whether the imposture were by means of 'lines' on the hand, or 'conjunctions of the stars'? What mattered was whether the imposture were carried on by means of a stupid boy or a cunning boy. If they were honestly and fairly deemed to be impostures, people had a right to say so, and he did not hesitate to say that he looked upon the plaintiff as one of the pests of society. When he found that Zadkiel was predicting other persons' deaths, and had not even shrunk from bringing into his balderdash the name of the illustrious and lamented prince whom we had lately lost, he acknowledged that he felt the deepest indignation — the more so as these pretended predictions were couched cunningly in terms of such artful vagueness that, in almost any event, they might be said to be verified. He wondered whether the prophet had consulted the stars as to the outcome of this trial, or whether Saturn was in the ascendant. (Laughter.)

Here the lord chief justice remarked wittily, 'I fancy he will think he is "in Scorpio".'

Mr Ballantine replied that he suspected Mr Morrison probably thought his 'bright particular star' was Serjeant Shee (laughter) and that he cared not a straw for any other 'conjunction' whatever. The plaintiff had predicted the deaths of Lord Palmerston and Lord Brougham, but happily they survived; and as to the former, no doubt he cared more for combinations in the House of Commons than for any 'conjunctions of stars'. (More laughter.) He contended that his client had a perfect right to denounce all this trash as imposture, and most mischievous and infamous imposture. Not the less so — but all the more so — because it appeared that some poor creatures fancied them to be true.

Passing on to the visions of biblical figures, Mr Ballantine denounced them as blasphemous and calculated to bring religion into contempt. The conversation or interview with Judas Iscariot, for instance: what could be more monstrous? And was it gravely to be heard, as a matter of defence, that these things might be true? As to their being done for profit, he did not believe that fortune-telling was a philanthropical institution (laughter) or that any other system of imposture ever was so. The jury might depend upon it that if there was an imposture, it was not for nothing. And the *Almanac*, in which mention was made of the ball and of 'advice' to persons of uneasy minds, was admitted to be for profit; so too the teaching of 'the aspects of the stars'. Who were these people whose 'minds were uneasy'? The weak and the valetudinarian, and those who would go to a conjurer when they had tired a doctor: such was the class of minds over whom this astrologer bore sway. Probably the jury could hardly think it possible that any persons could be so foolish as to be misled by these delusions.

As to the people of rank who had been called, they had merely beguiled a few idle hours, and it was really too bad to summon these ladies here when their husbands might as well have been called. As for the elderly lady who was called upon to prove the visions she had seen — really it was a pitiable spectacle and a marked illustration of the mischievous results of this system of fraud and imposture. That system his client, Sir Edward Belcher, had denounced with natural indignation, as became a sailor who had seen the wonders and the grandeur of nature in both hemispheres, and felt a natural detestation and disgust for these wretched tricks, which were only fit to put money into the pocket of an impostor. He stood by the right to repeat Sir Edward's expression of that opinion and he believed that he would have the sympathy of every thinking man. Indeed, he would not insult the good sense of the jury by imagining for one moment that they would give a verdict unfavourable to his client, a gentleman who had passed so many years of his life in endeavouring to add to the stock of knowledge his countrymen possessed.

Finally, the lord chief justice summed up. 'Gentlemen of the jury,' he began,

> the pith of the supposed libel is that the plaintiff, Mr Morrison, is an impostor and guilty of wilfully gulling the public. Now before you can find for the defendant, Sir Edward Belcher, you must be of the opinion firstly that the facts stated in the libel were true, and that the plaintiff exhibited the ball knowing it was an imposture; and secondly that he did it in order to get money.
>
> There are persons who, through obliquity of mind or prejudices, or passion, or delusion, bring themselves into a state in which they are imposed upon. And if the plaintiff himself really believes these revelations made by boys looking in a crystal, though you might laugh at him, can you really say he is an imposter? As for the latter part of the defence, there can be no doubt that the charge of exhibiting the ball for money has altogether failed. And the reception of money for the *Almanac*, or the teaching of astrology, or the casting of horoscopes: this will not support the plea of the reception of money for the exhibition of the ball. In short, it is one thing to be an impostor and another to be a fraudulent impostor. The plea of justification, therefore, is not made out.
>
> As to the other ground of defence, that the matter was one fit for public discussion and denunciation: if the system was mischievous, and calculated to delude the unwary and the credulous, it was, no doubt, fit subject for public denunciation. But it is another thing to say that because a man put forward such a publication or such a system, a public writer can therefore go back into his history and state facts which are not true,

and which are calculated to do him injury. His system might be described as an imposture, but facts must not be invented or misstated as to his past life, with a view to destroy the credit of it.

Sir Edward has taken it upon himself to say that the plaintiff, in his past life, has been guilty of wilful imposture, and for the purpose of profit. Therefore you must be satisfied, in order to find for him, not only that he honestly believed that the plaintiff had taken money for a fraudulent exhibition, but that he had such fair grounds for his imputation that his inference was not so unfair as to be reckless. It was true that the exhibition of the crystal ball had been so general as to be public; still, the personal character of the plaintiff was involved in the imputations made upon him, and unless they can be defended, either upon the grounds just stated or upon the plea of justification, then you must find for the plaintiff.

Thus far the lord chief justice's summing-up was no more than what had been expected: the application of a subtle and disinterested legal mind to the case in hand. Reporters were already scribbling down the revelation that it was one thing to be an impostor and another to be a fraudulent impostor. But now Sir Alexander continued, and with somewhat more animation:

Even in that case, however, it is clear that Sir Edward has written with an honest desire to put down what he deemed to be an imposture. And no doubt there is much that is reprehensible in it. With respect to the publication of *Zadkiel's Almanac* in particular, the matter becomes altogether of a very different nature, because I cannot help remarking that the publication of a volume of such a character lays the party doing so open to very severe criticism. I think there is a great deal in it of what is preposterous and mischievous, and an author imbued with the peculiarities of Zadkiel must expect to meet strictures of a not very pleasant nature. But then, even within such circumstances, those comments must be within the bounds of fair and honest criticism. You have heard the terms with which the author of the *Almanac* has been stigmatized, and you therefore will have to say how far he has suffered from those observations.

Looking at the price of *Zadkiel's Almanac*, however, and at the sort of stuff it contains, I think there is an imposition made. For example, a person might get an almanac for a halfpenny that would tell him the day of the month, and give him other useful information; but the plaintiff's almanac, filled with speculations about the conjunctions of the planets and their influence on people's fortunes and the affairs of this world, is priced sixpence, which is fivepence-and-halfpenny more than it is worth. [Laughter.] Now, I must say, that is an imposition upon the public.

Of all the strange delusions that had ever misled the mind of man, the notion that our destinies are affected by the combinations of stars is perhaps the strangest. Ancient astronomers affixed, for convenience, certain names to certain stars, borrowing those names from heathen mythology; and then astrologers actually, in their ignorance, ascribed to the stars the character of those deities whose names they bore. Then, because one bright star was called Venus and another of a more fiery red was called Mars, they fancied that persons born 'under' those stars had the characteristics of those particular heathen deities. Nothing could be more absurd, and such is the rubbish with which this almanac is filled.

The learned judge's imperfect grasp of history proving no impediment to his confidence, one imagines his discourse growing in power and authority until the court-room is reduced to a classroom filled with silent children, perhaps even Zadkiel struggling to retain his bearing.

How people can be led to believe that planets named after heathen deities can have influence upon their birth and fortunes is indeed surprising. It is absurd to entertain such opinions, and when those opinions lead to disturbance in the minds of persons, they become mischievous and often productive of evil consequences. The plaintiff in his *Almanac* of 1861, amongst other predictions, spoke of evil impending over the lamented Prince Consort. [Here the lord chief justice repeated Zadkiel's prediction.] I will now direct the attention of the jury to the month of October, when the Sun enters Scorpio. 'The chief feature of this month,' the author says, 'is "the great conjunction" on the 21st day . . . My own ascendant suffers by this phenomenon, and this may warn me that my star will soon set also; but I hope I may reflect without vanity that *vitae brevis est cursus, gloriae sempiternus* [the course of life is short, that of glory everlasting]. Mars, whose recent transit through Scorpio has disturbed Barbary, Syria, &c., as also Norway, now enters Libra, and therein he destroys the peace of Lisbon and of Austria, whose troubles arise; and in Old England the square of the Moon to Mars, in the Royal horoscope, brings violence and many national troubles. Wailing in high places. Louis Napoleon flourishes.' So much for Scorpio. What could be more absurd?

No wonder that a man so distinguished in the realms of science as Sir Edward Belcher should be led to denounce such a system. And if you think this partakes of the character of imposture, but you also think that in doing so he has stepped beyond the law, you are at liberty to consider the nature of the publication in your verdict as to the amount of damages you award. Gentlemen of the jury, I have now laid the case before you. You should consider the evidence and give your verdict accordingly.

The jury then retired. They were absent for an hour. Upon returning, they delivered their verdict: 'My Lord, we find the defendant guilty.'

'And what damages have you decided to award to the plaintiff?'

'Twenty shillings, Your Lordship.'

The lord chief justice then refused an application for both parties' costs.

Zadkiel had won his case, but like the Greek King Pyrrhus after defeating the Romans, he might have felt that another victory like this and we're done for. Although his astrology was incidental to the case he had brought, it proved — just as his counsel had feared and Belcher's had clearly decided from the outset — to be his weakest and most damning point. Encouraged by the judge, that opinion was confirmed by the derisory amount of damages awarded by the jury.

In fact, the case against Zadkiel outlined by the lord chief justice encapsulated virtually all the learned opposition to astrology of this and preceding centuries. It appealed to all the standard shibboleths: religious orthodoxy, as opposed to personal prophecy; safe scientific knowledge, as opposed to dangerous astral imposture; and, above all, 'common sense', as opposed to laughable, but arguably deranged, eccentricity.

Zadkiel was perhaps lucky to obtain a favourable verdict at all, but both the amount of damages and the ridicule he attracted during and after the trial were a hard blow. Yet the press too was unsatisfied at the outcome. *The Times* of two days later admitted:

> Perhaps what a bishop, a distinguished novelist, and many persons of rank had condescended to look at, an almanack-maker may be supposed to believe in, and, of course, he was entitled to the benefit of the doubt. Yet we must confess to a feeling that the Jury took the most lenient view of the matter possible ... While 'mediums' are tolerated, it would be hard to convict Mr Morrison of imposture. But it is a melancholy reflection ...

The *Saturday Review* of 4 July responded more robustly. In an editorial entitled 'Darkness in High Places', the writer concluded that 'The case of Morrison v. Belcher seems to display the existence among fashionable and educated people of an amount of credulity and superstition that we thought was confined to servant maids and village crones.' Though Zadkiel's astrology is an imposture, he himself goes free.

> All, therefore, we can say is, that the gipsies are hardly dealt with ... No gallant Admiral may say that the gallant Lieutenant has ever been guilty of imposture, at least of wilful imposture for the purposes of profit; but any police constable may arrest, and any magistrate convict to fine and imprisonment, the poor Pagan under the hedge whose belief in necromancy and stellar influences has descended to her through the traditions of two thousand years.

Needless to say, the writer was not advocating the logical conclusion to this line of reasoning, namely the repeal of the part of the Vagrancy Act criminalizing such beliefs. His purpose was rather to lament the fact that

> without much doubt, there are a million of English people who have some sort of confidence in Zadkiel, and the like of him. And certainly there is ample encouragement to them in the countenance afforded to Zadkiel by the many great, and wise, and learned of the land ... Anyhow,

the dupes who believe in Zadkiel are not more culpable than the fools who countenance him by their presence at his exhibitions. The curious thing to consider is, that this little revelation and the roaring trade which 'mediums' drive in England and America show that an age of reason and knowledge is also an age of abject credulity and stupid superstition . . . Religion began in fetichism, and in fetichism it seems likely to end; and the rites of fetichism are not likely to be unpopular if bishops and dignitaries are to be found in the congregation of the necromancer.

Very shortly after the trial, Christopher Cooke published his last book, *Curiosities of Occult Literature*, in which he finally settled his accounts with astrology and Zadkiel. His only justification for his involvement with it, he wrote, 'was the testing of the truth of the astrological principle; and if this principle was to be plainly denied . . . all my thirteen years' work was labour lost'. Not surprisingly for a solicitor, he interpreted the failure of his and Zadkiel's efforts to alter the law as just such a denial. Despite the latter's assurances to the contrary, 'persons of education and of good standing in society' had proved unwilling to support astrology.

Cooke admitted that, as a result of accepting Zadkiel's inflated estimate of its standing in society, he had seriously underestimated his own 'losses, annoyances, and general detriment' in its pursuit. Now the Ancient Mariner of Victorian occultism, Cooke concluded that

> Unless, therefore, persons are pretty well settled in life, and sufficiently free to be independent of public men generally, it appears that the less they have at present to do with Astrology, Phrenology, or Spiritualism — all tabooed subjects, on account of their truth — the better it will be for their reputations, liberty of action, and the state of their pockets.

Cooke tried to understand the reasons for his failure. 'In Britain,' he speculated,

> we have the element of *caste* to a greater extent, perhaps, than in any other country; and if it should be proved that the various gradations of rank do depend on stellar influences . . . there would be a qualification of the famous hero-worship in which some persons delight, and the dimensions

of which would be gall and wormwood to their souls.

Astrology might even cast doubt on the right or ability of a particular monarch to reign,

> hence, presuming that the theory is true, we see the serious doctrines it would introduce, and the reason why it is regarded with suspicion by the authorities. It is only on account of this reason that I can understand the treatment to which persons, including myself, have been personally subjected.

It is doubtful whether astrology's Victorian critics would have explained their hostility to astrology in quite this way but, as if to underscore Cooke's warning to those considering a career in astrology, virtually the only recognition of his final efforts was a sour review in the *Athenaeum* of 11 July 1863, beginning: 'While the country is laughing at the pretensions of Lieutenant Zadkiel, a few idle persons will perhaps like to turn over the pages of this weary, dreary, inexplicable little book.'

Zadkiel too refused to have anything more to do with Cooke, presumably feeling that too much dirty linen had been washed in public. He even died, as Cooke peevishly noted, 'without noticing the book in any manner' and owing him £128. 'The case and this volume,' Cooke concluded rather belatedly, 'prove the necessity for caution in all business matters, especially in dealing with plausible or dubious persons who affect philanthropy.' With that, Cooke retired from public and professional life. He died on 18 April 1882. A life-long bachelor, he left his considerable income to be divided among his nephews and nieces, apart from endowing an annual prize at Harrow, which is still awarded, for proficiency in English.

As for Zadkiel, after the trial we hear little more from him. The second volume of his last astrological textbook, *The Hand-book of Astrology*, appeared that year and, five years later, another instalment of his astronomy, modestly entitled *The New Principia, or, True System of Astronomy*. In 1872, he again approached three members of Parliament about amending Section 4 of the Vagrancy Act. All three declined, putting a full stop to that crusade. Most of his subsequent energy seems to have gone into his almanac, believing that giving a copy to another reader was now practically the only way to further the cause of astrology, 'since the doors of the Press remain closed against it, with scarcely an exception'. That was written in 1870; the following year, Charles Kent, the sympathetic editor of the *Sun* and virtually the sole exception, retired.

Sales of the almanac continued to grow, however: according to Zadkiel's own published estimates, up 3,000 copies after the trial to 58,000 for 1864. By 1870 he was selling about 80,000 copies a year. The character of *Zadkiel's Almanac* was still unmistakably that of its author, a robust mix of stentorian editorials and daring predictions. Even the *London Review* admitted: 'There is a tone of plain-spoken accuracy about some parts of the writing which stamps either the audacious or the honest man.' And Zadkiel carried on the tradition of the odd striking 'hit' — infuriating coincidence to the critic, astonishing prophecy to the convinced — which arguably any astrologer worth his or her salt should occasionally be able to manage. Writing in the summer of 1864, *Zadkiel's Almanac* forecast the ending of hostilities in the American Civil War, based on the lunar eclipse of 10 April 1865, set for Washington D.C. He wrote:

> I regret to see that some fighting will still go on; yet the slaves are seen to be freed, and the nature of the quarrel will be entirely altered; and, after the month of May, it seems to die out by sheer exhaustion ... I find Jupiter strong in the Ascendant, which *will render the people pacific and reasonable, and disposed to peace, which, I have no doubt, will take place under the benefic influence of this Eclipse.*

Robert E. Lee surrendered to General Grant on the day of the eclipse itself and the last Confederate army followed suit on 26 May.

Ten years later, Zadkiel might again have felt cheered. On 13 May 1873, the *Daily Telegraph* reported that miners had gone on strike in North Wales as a result of his prediction of 'combustions and underground troubles'. 'On the 10th and 11th of May,' he had written, 'Mars will form an evil aspect with Saturn and Uranus; this denotes violent explosions in mines and numerous deaths thereby.' Some perverse satisfaction ensued, perhaps, when a mining explosion on that date in Nova Scotia cost several lives.

By now Zadkiel had moved to 'Sunnyside', a house in the quiet suburban street of Knight's Park in Kingston-upon-Thames. He died there on 5 February 1874 of heart disease. In his will, Zadkiel bequeathed his beloved 'magic crystal' to his eldest son Robert. He was quickly accorded the ultimate honour, among astrologers, of literary semi-immortality. R.V. Sparkes, who was also Raphael V, inherited his mantle first, but died the next year; whereupon another astrologer from London, Alfred J. Pearce, became Zadkiel III. As we shall see, Pearce made *Zadkiel's Almanac* his own and took its sales past 100,000 before he died in 1923. The almanac survived until 1931, succumbing just before a new wave of popular newspaper astrology hit the streets.

CHAPTER IV

A.J. PEARCE AND RICHARD GARNETT: A PAGAN SCIENCE

I N 1861, A YOUNG MAN OF twenty-one joined Morrison's Astro-Meteo-rological Society. The following year, he sent in his first contribution to *Zadkiel's Almanac* and, the year after, burning his bridges behind him, published his own *Defence and Exposition of the Principles of Astrology*.

This young Turk was Alfred James Pearce, who was presumably not receiving the shrewdest advice about promising career moves in contemporary England; not from his father, at any rate. In a famous trial, C.T. Pearce, a member of the Royal College of Surgeons, was acquitted of manslaughter on 27 October 1849, after a patient whom he was treating for cholera died. The key point is that Dr Pearce was a homoeopath, and the charge was brought by Thomas Wakley, a medical reformer, member of Parliament and the first editor of *The Lancet*. Wakley campaigned tirelessly for truth, reason and middle-class professional power and, as far as we know, never wasted much time on self-doubt. The defendant's counsel concluded that 'this indictment is merely an attack upon the homoeopathic system' and the jury evidently agreed.

Dr Pearce was also interested in medical astrology and he carefully recorded the time of his son's birth: 9.20 a.m. on 10 November 1840, at 13 King William Street, London W.C. (Using the dates of the major events in his life, Pearce later 'corrected' this time to 9.18.39 a.m. Such a procedure, called 'rectification', represented a challenge astrologers have rarely felt able to resist.) The young Pearce absorbed both his father's commitment to homoeopathy and his hostility to vivisection and compulsory vaccination and, by the age of twenty, he too was studying astrology. He began a medical degree at University College London, but this was thwarted by insufficient funds; so, in 1869, he followed his father's general practice to Sunderland as an unqualified medical assistant. Whenever possible, Dr Pearce would require his son's astral diagnosis and prescription for each case in advance of delivering his own medical one.

In February 1874, Zadkiel died; and, in May the next year, so too did his immediate successor as editor of *Zadkiel's Almanac*, R. V. Sparkes. The Morrison family asked A. J. Pearce to step in. Accepting the position, he returned to London with his family in May and settled in Wandsworth. He had married a lively young Frenchwoman, Léonie Rieder and had five surviving children. The die was cast and Pearce went on to become the grand old man of late Victorian astrology. By the time he died in 1923, aged eighty-two, he had edited *Zadkiel's Almanac* for forty-seven years, five more than his namesake; he had also produced the last authoritative manual of the century, *The Textbook of Astrology*, in two volumes, 1879 and 1889, and reprinted in 1911.

Above all, Pearce fought the good fight on the two fronts that have so often preoccupied astrologers in the public eye and which we first encountered with Raphael: colleagues who are letting the side down, and outside enemies from the world of letters and learning. In both campaigns, his resolution never once wavered: astrology was above all an applied mathematical science. In particular, Pearce adopted a complex method of advancing nativities in time to predict future conditions, if not events, known as 'primary directions', and damned any other astrologer (the majority) who settled for the much simpler method of 'secondary directions'. Such internecine disputes make no more sense to the uninitiated than do struggles between Maoists and Trotskyists or Baptists and Evangelicals. None are more bitter, however, and the reason is that the nicety in question is always emblematic of some larger claim. In this case, rejection of his beloved primary directions was sufficient for Pearce to identify a mystically inclined, mathematically incompetent impostor.

In this stance, while remaining loyal to his mentor Zadkiel the astrologer, Pearce parted company from Zadkiel the seer, warning his readers: 'We draw the line at magic and spiritualism.' Instead, in 1877 for example, he offered them a digest of Francis Galton's latest work on heredity. The audience for a more sober-sided *Zadkiel's Almanac* must have changed character somewhat, but the circulation does not seem to have suffered: 150,000 purchasers in 1863 and holding steady throughout the 1870s and '80s.

Pearce's enemy within was theosophical astrology (see Chapter V). For two decades, from their public appearance in the 1890s, he was among their bitterest critics, accusing them of 'misleading students who are induced to begin under their tuition, and bringing astrology into disrepute. The superstitious nonsense taught in "Modern Astrology" and certain "Guides"' — the publications of Alan Leo and Robert T. Cross (Raphael VI) respectively — 'is nauseating.' In terms that might have come straight from the pens of astrology's mainstream critics, he held that 'The best writers on astrology do not pander to the tastes of the vulgar, nor encourage the superstitions of the ignorant.' His own work, he declared, was intended solely for 'the intelligent and highly educated portion of the community'.

At the same time, Pearce struggled manfully against the spokesmen of just that portion of the community who regarded the whole subject, his own contribution included, as indefensible. At this time they were led by R. A. Proctor, a popular science writer and astronomer in the mould of the polemicists for the SDUK, and Sir David Brewster, an eminent scientist who used his position as editor of the *Edinburgh Cyclopedia* to attack astrology while simultaneously insisting that it was already long dead. Pearce used his own books and almanac to reply, although with as little effect as his opponents had on him.

But, as usual, matters were not as simple as they appeared. The scientific establishment itself was divided, and the natural objects whose interpretation it had long contested with astrologers — the Sun, Moon and planets — continued to generate intense internal controversy. In a series of influential articles in the late 1860s, a prominent physicist, Balfour Stewart, together with J. Norman Lockyer, the first editor of the journal *Nature*, drew on the observations of sun-spots at Kew Observatory to argue that rather than an inanimate machine, the universe resembled a giant organism, suffused with a guiding spiritual dimension. 'There seems to be a great molecular delicacy of construction in the sun,' they wrote, 'and probably also, to an inferior extent, in the various planets . . . *The result of all this will be that a disturbance from without is very easily communicated to our luminary, and that when it takes place it communicates a thrill to the very extremities of the system.*' (This passage ought to have a familiar ring in the context of current arguments over the Earth as a living organism, the universe as a quasi-spiritual hologram or a Taoist dancing master, and so on. These are clearly perennial themes.)

When the question of funding for the Kew Observatory came up at the Royal Astronomical Society, it was Proctor, whose keen nose detected the whiff of astral heresy, who led the opposition. In Stewart and Lockyer's new 'physics of astronomy', he wrote to a friend in 1872, 'solar physics and solar photography become the leading features — and *they* are associated with the preposterous idea (worthy of Zadkiel and the editor of Moore's Almanac) that the phenomena of weather may one day be predicted from the records of solar spots, faculae, and prominences!'

Pearce won some grudging respect for his rigour, at least. The *Athenaeum*, reviewing his *Textbook of Astrology* on 14 June 1879, conceded that 'his work shows that [astrology's] practice requires some degree of education and of labour, for its methods are founded on astronomical calculations'; and even that 'As astrology stands it is a more respectable science than Spiritualism.' The anonymous writer's response, however, was simply to raise the requirements for admission to the club. He also demanded more evidence: 'What we want from Mr Pearce or from Zadkiel is a chronology or almanac of the future, not the past, life of the Prince of Wales; a scheme showing when he will win the Derby, when he will lay a foundation-stone, and all the important political events of his career until the exact day of his death.' At the same time, however, what was apparently needed was a better theory: 'Neither Mr Pearce nor any of his brethren . . . explains on what scientific grounds one planet is a she, and another is the orb of war . . . This lies at the root of astrology, and all the calculations that can be put forward will not supply a demonstration.'

By now, for his part, Pearce may have realized that he was being toyed with; and possibly even that his own claims for astrology as a predictive science opened him up to just some of the impossible demands being made. Nor did he really succeed in carrying the debate forward. In correspondence carried in *The Lancet* in 1913-14, when Pearce was allowed to entertain its readers by arguing for medical astrology, he cited the seventeenth-century examples of Bacon and Kepler — not exactly a fresh or original contribution.

Ironically, writing in 1909 he went some way towards meeting one of the *Athenaeum*'s strictures. In his almanac for the following year, he stated: 'If the King's physicians would pay attention to astrological science, they would not advise His Majesty to travel abroad either this spring or summer, in view of the first, fourth, and seventh of the primary directions operating this year.' On 7 March 1910, Edward VII caught a chill on his way to stay in Biarritz; complications set in, and he died on 7 May. In marked contrast to Zadkiel I's first successful foray into royal prediction, however, this one met with stony indifference. There was undoubtedly less self-confidence now among the ruling British élites compared with fifty years earlier. Perhaps, therefore, although the ruling opinion was no more favourable towards astrology, it was more tolerant of transgressions.

Pearce died on 25 April 1923. He was buried in Wandsworth Cemetery in south London. At eighty-two, he had survived into an era that must have felt like a foreign country. None the less, he never compromised his moral and mathematical vision of astrology. Just as much as those louder voices claiming to represent the age, his voice too — so late Victorian in its tone, if unfamiliar in content — deserves its place in history.

The circular Reading Room of the British Library, at the heart of the British Museum in Bloomsbury, is famous for such readers as

Thomas Carlyle, Karl Marx and George Bernard Shaw. It has long nour-
ished many lesser-known hierophants of knowledge at least as exotic,
however, if less influential. For more than a century, the Reading Room,
together with the bookshops, cafés and meeting-rooms in the generous
shadow of its great dome, have succoured generations of occultists,
magicians and theosophists, as well as their more antiquarian colleagues
and the merely curious. It seems fitting, therefore, that in February
1879, Richard Garnett — the Superintendent of the Reading Room, and
by general acclaim its presiding genius in the last quarter of the nineteenth century — called A. J. Pearce over to the centre desk and warmly
congratulated him on his *Textbook*, published the previous month.

Garnett was born in Lichfield, at 5.51 p.m. on 27 February
1835, into middle-class circumstances and a literary and erudite
family. Taken together, the members of the Garnett family constitute,
in the words of one biographer, 'an intellectual aristocracy', a tradition
that has continued down through Garnett's daughter-in-law Constance,
grandson David and great-grandson Richard, among others.

From childhood onwards, Garnett read prodigiously and before
long mastered at least six foreign languages. At sixteen, he went
to work as a book 'placer' in the bowels of the British Museum.
His extraordinary memory, general knowledge and skills as a librarian
were finally recognized in 1875, when he became Superintendent of the
Reading Room. In the course of his stay, he was entrusted with the production of the first general catalogue, still in use. Fifteen years later, he
succeeded to the position of Keeper of Printed Books and left his house
on Primrose Hill to take up residence in the Librarian's House, part of
the right-hand wing of the British Museum. When Garnett retired after
forty-eight years of service in 1899, it was to the general plaudits of the
English-speaking world of letters. He accrued a pretty wide range of
honours, including both a portrait of Karl Marx, gratefully inscribed,
and a C.B. (Companion of the Order of the Bath).

Yet, from the age of twenty-five, to the amazement and incredu-
lity of his family and friends, Garnett had been a serious student of
astrology. As he wrote to Pearce, 'I was led by a sudden impulse received

on January 29 1861, at about a quarter to eleven in the forenoon, and at
the precise moment when Mercury, then in *Aquarius*, came to the trine
aspect with Uranus, which had for some time been *stationary* near my
Mid-Heaven.' This makes perfect sense to an astrologer. Mercury, the
messenger of the gods, signifies the mind; Uranus was suspected by
many of its nineteenth-century practitioners of having a special affinity
with astrology; and a 'trine' aspect of 120° felicitously connects any
planets at either end. Both men were struck by the coincidence that, as
they soon discovered, Pearce had begun his own life-long astral studies
only eight months earlier.

It is hard to say how generally Garnett's predilection was known.
When writing on astrology, he appeared in print as A. G. Trent, an
anagram of his surname. On the other hand, he never made a secret of
his interest; quite the contrary. For example, in 1862, he wrote to *The
Spectator*, which on 22 February published a summary of his letter and
its own bemused reaction, beginning thus:

> We thought we had done with Astrology, but an opponent far more
> redoubtable than Zadkiel has now taken up the cudgels, and challenged
> us by our reputation for candour to publish his unanswerable facts. He
> sends his name, is obviously an educated, thoughtful man, who can argue
> temperately, and in excellent English, and he believes Astrology to be an
> exact science. We regret that we have no room for his letter, but unlike
> the majority of crotchety intellects, who believe, or affect to believe in
> astrology, he attempts to produce a body of evidence, and his 'proofs'
> are curious enough to deserve quotation.

The body of evidence which Garnett produced was the history of the later
Bourbons: nineteen nativities in all, and all with one exception 'derived
from official documents, which anyone who pleases may inspect at the
British Museum'. As his list showed in some detail, they shared, by aspect
and position, a heavy burden of the traditional 'malefic' planets Mars and
Saturn as well as unpredictable Uranus, with corresponding ill-fortune in
life for all except two, who had escaped these astral afflictions at birth.
'In other words,' commented *The Spectator*, 'the only faith for mankind

is a belief in destiny, and that a blind destiny . . . ' But the writer was under no illusions that such a caustic conclusion settled the matter:

> We laugh at the silly girl who believes that a stupid tramp can predict her future from the lines on her hand, but of the hundreds who may read G.'s list of Bourbon nativities, half will secretly doubt whether there may not be something in a science which, if it be a sound one, condemns about a fourth of the human race to an ill luck against which energy is powerless and character no safeguard.

In a manner reminiscent of John Varley, few of Garnett's friends seem to have escaped an unsolicited astral analysis. When Garnett was first introduced to Ralph Shirley, the editor of *The Occult Review*, he remarked, 'I think I can tell you what sign of the zodiac you were born under', and specified Scorpio. When asked how he had known, Garnett replied that the expression of Shirley's eyes was his principal clue.

Samuel Butler, author of the utopian satire *Erewhon* and the iconoclastic novel *The Way of All Flesh*, provided another subject. On 28 June 1883, Butler wrote to his father to ask him his time of birth. 'My reason for asking,' he explained,

> is this. My friend Mr Garnett of the British Museum has, or pretends to have, a craze about astrology. I suppose he is not serious, but I really do not know what to think. I saw him this morning and said I was not well; I caught a cold from a wetting two or three days ago and was yesterday laid up, but am out and about as usual today. He said: 'How curious! I was afraid you might be ill and was thinking of writing to enquire.'
>
> I asked why. He rather hummed and ha'd, and at length explained that, if I was born in the latter part of December 4 1835, I should be suffering from the transit (I think he said transit) of Saturn, as the Queen and two or three more people were. If, however, I was born in the early part of the day, it would not affect me.

Butler's father, replying that he could not remember what time his son had been born, asked about Garnett's interest. In response, Butler complained:

> I can never understand why Mr Garnett flirts with astrology. He is a superintendent of the Reading Room of the British Museum and is certainly the best informed man I ever met ... in fact, he is perhaps the most extraordinary man — as far as knowledge of all sorts goes — that I have ever met ... I am afraid astrology is the one point in which he is vulnerable; for that he has a hankering after a bona fide belief that 'it has, at any rate, a foundation in science' is indisputable.

Nor were members of Garnett's own family exempt. When his grandson David was born on 9 March 1892 after a difficult pregnancy and birth, Garnett did not help matters by commissioning a horoscope by one James R. Wallace, also known as 'Mercury', of Halifax. (Astrologers sometimes ask colleagues to supply interpretations when they feel too close to the person concerned to retain their objectivity of judgement.) The result was a very gloomy affair, promising all manner of difficulties thanks to the position of Saturn, which the parents fortunately laughed off.

Even Butler — an unusually open-minded man, and one predisposed to sympathize with Garnett — could only consider his passion for astrology an inexplicable 'craze', and possibly even merely 'pretended'. Others arrived at their own explanations. The scientist and spiritualist Alfred Russell Wallace, co-founder with Darwin of evolutionary theory, offered one that Garnett himself would have firmly rejected. After the latter's death, Wallace recalled:

> I am quite satisfied that there *are* astrologers who do give very striking readings of *character* and sometimes of *events*. I may say I knew Mr Garnett ... My conclusion is that the care, attention, labour and study required to draw out accurate *results*, offer the *conditions* which enable spirits to impress on the astrological student the results he gets or thinks he gets from the complexities of the figures. The astrologer is in fact a medium.

Of course, what people find amazing and incomprehensible is, so to speak, highly relative. Just when Garnett's astrology was thought so provocative, the Society for Psychical Research — committed to proving scientifically the reality of spiritualism and psychic powers —

was being formed in 1882 by men such as Henry Sidgwick (Professor of Moral Philosophy at Cambridge), William Crookes (later President of the Royal Society) and among other eminent physicists Sir Oliver Lodge. During its first decade, it had no trouble in attracting the patronage of Gladstone, Ruskin and Tennyson. A. R. Wallace was another member.

As the various efforts to explain it imply, however, Garnett's astrology was harder to dismiss out of hand than that of a rank outsider like Zadkiel or Pearce. When empire and industry were still bearing powerful witness to the values of reason, fact and the material world, and other attempts to feed what those values left starved were so much more fashionable than astrology, the question remains: how could such an 'educated, thoughtful man' have taken it seriously?

As Butler feared, Garnett's involvement was no mere flirtation. The soil was his enquiring mind and the wealth of resources available to it, together with the intellectual independence of the self-taught. But it really began with his scholar's intuition — again, like Varley — that astrology offered a key to ancient mythology. However, he soon came to emulate rather than simply to analyse those authors whose astrology he hoped would unlock the ancient mind. To appreciate how this was possible, let us turn to his essay, first published in *The University Magazine* in 1880, entitled 'The Soul and the Stars'.

Like Pearce, Garnett insists on 'the strictly empirical character of astrology'. Despite being commonly considered 'as a kind of wizard', the astrologer

> works, as it were, under the surveillance of his brother the astronomer, and cannot falsify his data without instant detection. The principles of his art have come down to him in essentials from the most remote antiquity; they have been published in a thousand books, and are open to the examination of all the world. His calculations are performed by no more cabbalistical process than arithmetic. The influences he attributes to the heavenly bodies may be imaginary, but are in no sense *occult*, unless *occult* means *that which is not generally admitted*.

Garnett then examines the nativities of examples of the mentally ill, religious enthusiasts, criminals and eminent matches, such as Victoria and Albert, and Goethe and his mistress Christiane Vulpius, in a loosely statistical way. He concludes:

> There is nothing occult or mystical in the line of argument we have been pursuing. We have appealed throughout to the testimony of facts, partly notorious and indisputable facts of history and biography, and partly astronomical observations derived from no more recondite source than the ordinary ephemeris. Anyone can verify or disprove these observations in a moment by the same process.

Garnett's hostility to occult astrology was emphatic and he repeated it elsewhere. In 1901, he wrote:

> Nothing — unless it be the ill-advised attempt to predict the future with mathematical accuracy, and its connection in the popular mind with the species of fortune-telling called horary astrology — has brought scientific astrology into such disrepute as the notion that is is 'an occult science'. It is nothing of the kind . . . [and] could not be more grossly misrepresented than by being connected in any way with magic or theosophy.

He goes on to note that astrologers of the latter school 'have obtained attention, indeed, but by no means of a flattering nature'. And just after Garnett's death, a friend recalled: 'If there was one word he detested most frankly, it was "esoteric".'

Garnett stressed the need for co-operation between astrology and science, particularly the theory of heredity: 'Our contention is that the two theories complete each other, the latter accounting for the element of stability, the former for the element of variability.' But, to some extent, however understandably, he was deceiving himself. 'Facts', let alone theories, are far from being as straightforward and public as scientists often proclaim them to be. Garnett may thus also unintentionally deceive the reader; for his fundamental allegiance was not to modern science, but to ancient myth and philosophy.

That allegiance underlies most of Garnett's writings, whether his astrological essays or his *Lives* of Shelley, Emerson, Blake and Milton —

revealing choices, since they are virtually a litany of religious and social free-thinkers. It especially animates two of his other books: *The Twilight of the Gods and Other Tales*, published in 1888, which lovingly retells various stories from European and Asian mythology; and *De Flagello Myrteo. Thought and Fancies on Love*, a collection of coolly classical reflections on love and sex which was published anonymously in 1905 and is remarkably free of prudery or prurience. Like Varley, Garnett was evidently a modern pagan, agnostic at best towards Christianity, polytheistic at heart, and rational and empirical — but in a way that owed more to Aristotle and Plato than to Newton or Darwin. In the words of a biographer, 'Garnett lived as though the tight class structure of the Victorian world did not exist.' He treated its tight intellectual structure the same way.

It is thus not surprising that Garnett should have fallen for the stars once the ancient world had introduced them. The cosmologies of Ptolemy, Aristotle and Galen, with their all-important sub-lunar elements and humours, were steeped in astrology. With myth in his heart and philosophy in his head, then, Garnett, like Pearce, would have honestly denied any imputation of irrationality.

But something had changed in the half-century since Varley. Echoed in Garnett's fondness for prediction, 'against which energy is powerless and character no safeguard', the change is perceptible in his adoption, much more than Varley, of the rhetoric of contemporary science – its claims, tools and flourishes — and his corresponding antagonism to its ancient and inseparable enemy, magic. I have already suggested that, albeit in good company, Garnett was naïve. He was led by his own faith in reason to take them at their word when scientists and their votaries claimed that mantle as their own. (Ironically, Butler was one of his few educated contemporaries to perceive their own potential for arrogant dogmatism.) Thus Garnett was not, after all, altogether exempt from the tightly drawn lines of his time.

Around the turn of the century, he was asked to write the article on astrology for the forthcoming eleventh edition of the *Encyclopedia Britannica*. It is a great pity that after delaying, due to the pressure of other work, he died — in the early morning of 13 April 1906, at his home in Hampstead — before doing so. Perhaps he thought he had a little longer; on 10 December 1904, he had written to a fellow astrologer: 'The directions and transits in my nativity towards the end of 1906 are certainly very serious, my doubt is whether they will influence health or affairs.' He was buried in Highgate Cemetery.

Instead of Garnett's entry, the next edition of the *Encyclopedia* contained a virtual reprint of the article from the ninth edition: another tedious and hackneyed diatribe on 'ancient error' and its incomprehensible survival despite numerous 'death blows', by Morris Jastrow, Professor of Semitic Languages at the University of Pennsylvania. Garnett's contribution might have changed few professors' minds, but it would at least have opened a window on the subject and let in some fresh air.

Garnett was in obvious ways unique. As a self-taught scholar, he was succeeded by the university-educated professional librarian, a very different type. Nor is the latter likely to be enamoured of astrology. And it may be, when the British Library is installed at St Pancras and its august if unintentional patronage departs, the occult, magical and astral arts in Bloomsbury will wither. If so, London will be a duller place. Nevertheless, I find it hard to believe that there will be no more gentle and learned astrologers who have shaken the dust of recent millennia from their feet, and returned in spirit to a world where gods and goddesses still live among the stars.

CHAPTER V

ALAN LEO: FROM THE STARS TO THE STREET

T HE GREAT BETRAYER OF ASTROLOGY, according to Pearce and Garnett, seems at first blush a pretty innocuous character. He was portrayed at work, sometime around 1900, thus:

> It was a hot day in June. Seated before a roll-top desk in an upstairs
> room, the window of which opened out into a conservatory, in a large
> house in one of the Northern suburbs of London, was Albanus Leon ...
> He was a short thickset man of some forty summers, possessing an open
> countenance, hair turned slightly grey, and a pair of small steel grey eyes
> which always twinkled when he spoke. There was an air of dignity
> about his personality, which tended to make him somewhat proud and
> self-important, but on the other hand he possessed much geniality and
> there was a certain magnetism about his presence which had a soothing
> influence on all around him.
>
> The morning mail had just been delivered, and Albanus Leon was
> busily engaged in sorting out a large pile of letters of all shapes and
> sizes ... Most of them contained money orders, for Leon had an immense
> clientele, and the income from his business had now reached four figures a
> year and bid fair to greatly increase as time went on. The mail this morning
> was an exceptionally heavy one and the pile of postal and money orders
> was rapidly mounting up.

The writer, E. H. Bailey, had been until two years earlier an employee of 'Albanus Leon', or to use his proper adopted name, Alan Leo. Bailey's picture rings true, if a touch acerbic, but it is potentially misleading — Leo's geniality masked a formidable will and his profits went for the most part straight back into his business. The latter was the publicity machine for his life-mission, which he announced in 1895, declaring: 'The time has come to modernise the ancient system of Astrology.' And to a remarkable extent, he succeeded. Modern astrology is difficult to imagine without his intervention. That Leo's idea of modernity gave pride of place to a revivified 'Wisdom–Religion' may seem bizarre, of course, but it made perfect sense to him and his considerable, and by no means uneducated, following in early twentieth-century London. Indeed, it is with us still.

Alan Leo was born William Frederick Allen at 6.10 a.m. on 7 August 1860 in Great College Street, just behind Westminster Abbey. His mother was a dedicated member of the Plymouth Brethren, a tiny but ferocious Protestant sect; his father was a Scottish ex-soldier, who soon tired of his wife's religious fanaticism and disappeared when Leo was about nine. Neither parent was wealthy, and from the age of sixteen Leo was obliged to fend for himself, working variously as a draper, chemist's assistant, grocer, sewing machine salesman and shop manager. His professional fortunes varied enormously — a fact he attributed to the presence of Uranus in the tenth house of his nativity — and these jobs alternated with bouts of unemployment and poverty. They also ran in tandem with what seems to have been an unrelated inner life, perhaps impelled by his mother's religiosity. He had rejected that, but retained a lifelong concern with the larger questions of life.

Leo first became interested in astrology when he was about eighteen. At twenty-one, while managing a grocery shop, he was treated for a minor complaint by one Dr Richardson, a herbalist–astrologer in Nottingham, from whom he learned more. Four years later, now the manager of an engineering firm in London, he encountered the concept of reincarnation. By the age of twenty-eight, Leo wrote later, 'I had plunged very deeply into the private study of Natal Astrology.' He had also learned about the idea of karma — roughly, a chain of cause-and-effect whereby one's present actions determine one's future nature and circumstances, just as one's past actions, which may or may not include those of previous lives, have already determined those of one's present. Undoubtedly it was this discovery that led him to a closer involvement with Theosophy.

We have already encountered Madame Blavatsky as a young woman in London, hungry for a glimpse of her favourite author, Sir Edward Bulwer-Lytton. Since then she had travelled far, absorbing mystical and occult philosophies, and arousing fascination and denunciation in about equal measure. In 1875, together with Colonel Henry Olcott, she founded the Theosophical Society in New York. Two years later, she published *Isis Unveiled: A Master Key to the Mysteries of Ancient and Modern Science and Theology*. This was succeeded in 1888 by *The Secret Doctrine: The Synthesis of Science, Religion and Philosophy*. These *monstres sacrés* were made up of a mass of Neo-platonism, Hermeticism, Gnosticism, magic, alchemy and astrology, topped up with a hefty dollop of Hinduism and Buddhism. Much of it was attributed to the 'Mahatmas', a spiritually evolved brotherhood living in the Himalayas, contact with which, or even membership of, was the ambition of every Theosophical novitiate.

Scholarly criticisms that Blavatsky's work was derivative and erroneous had little impact on its appeal. Indeed, its success was partly due to its being so turgidly complex that it offered something for almost everyone, and so deliberately comprehensive that its invented or re-invented terms (all the important ones) could only be checked against other firmly internal elements. In this sense, Blavatsky provided a model for many succeeding occultists, from Alice Baily to L. Ron Hubbard.

But there were other powerful appeals: more than a hint of Eastern promise, for example, for the jaded and cosmopolitan. Reincarnation and karma were central to Blavatsky's theory of human evolution, and she daringly pooh-poohed the uniqueness of both Christ and Christianity. At the same time, she also attacked scientific materialism, arguing that while the 'exoteric' scientist is limited to the study of nature's exterior, only spiritual perception can penetrate her inner mysteries. To many late Victorians, worried about the impact of scientific and especially

Darwinian beliefs, this sounded just the right note. However different their suggested solutions, such worries were also a major impetus to the Society of Psychical Research, as it continued to garner members from the *crème de la crème* of British scientific, political and social leaders.

In the words of Max Beerbohm; 'For those who like this sort of thing, this is the sort of thing they like.' Many did. The T.S., as the Theosophical Society was known, together with its colourful founder 'H. P. B.', set the pattern for virtually all such subsequent societies and sects, and in that sense its influence extended well beyond the 100,000 or so members world-wide that existed by the late 1880s.

A London Lodge of the T.S. had opened for business opposite the British Museum in 1878, led by A. P. Sinnett. Brisk sales of Sinnett's *The Occult World* in 1884 revealed a receptive audience for these daring 'new' ideas. It was not until the spring of 1887, however, when Blavatsky herself arrived on the scene, that Theosophy in London really took off. Settling in at 17 Lansdowne Road in Holland Park, the property of a wealthy follower which now became her 'lamasery' (as in the abode of a Tibetan lama), she quickly opened her own 'Blavatsky Lodge of the T.S.' in preference to the original group. It was no contest; the glamour of the former soon prevailed and it became a magnet for both the relatively committed — mesmerists, spiritualists, magicians, etc. — and the curious. The latter included an impressive array of urban gentry and *haute bourgeoisie*, especially, but by no means only, middle-aged to elderly wealthy and titled ladies. Among those who joined was the poet W. B. Yeats, who had just moved to London. Yeats's uncle, John Varley Jr, was already a Theosophist.

The vice-president of the Blavatsky Lodge, and a member of the coveted 'Inner Circle' — one of twelve members, to be precise — was a young astrologer named Walter Richard Old. He renamed himself W. Gorn Old and Blavatsky nick-named him 'The Astral Tramp', on account, she said, of his habit of 'roaming about in his astral body at night'. But he was best known by his astrological *nom de plume*, 'Sepharial', borrowed from yet another Hebrew angel. In the small circle of metropolitan astrologers, he and Leo met soon after the latter had moved to London; and it was Sepharial who introduced Leo to the Theosophical gatherings led by Blavatsky in Lansdowne Road during the summer of 1889.

The following May, Leo formally joined the T.S. and remained a devoted member for the rest of his life. He overlapped briefly with Yeats, who resigned that same year and joined the Hermetic Order of the Golden Dawn instead. Unlike the T.S., this was a small and secretive organization, which for two years from 1898 included the notorious magician Aleister Crowley. However, its co-founder, Dr W. W. Westcott, was a colleague of Sepharial's in H.P.B.'s Inner Circle. Both groups were part of the explosion of occultism and magic in England in the late 1880s and '90s. It was neither the first nor the last outbreak, of course, being reminiscent of the Swedenborgianism, Behemism and millenarianism of the 1780s and '90s; and not at all dissimilar, in our own time, to the renaissance of astrology, magic and interest in Eastern philosophies during the late 1960s and '70s.

Sepharial was an interesting person and a noteworthy astrologer in his own right. Born into relatively comfortable circumstances at about 1.30 a.m. on 20 March 1864 at Richmond House in Handsworth, Birmingham, he seems, in the words of a contemporary, to have 'arrived here with a very strong bias, which early led him to the study of occultism and allied subjects'. After an education at King Edward's School in Birmingham, he tore through Hebrew and the Cabbalah, Swedenborg, alchemy, Sanskrit and the Western magical tradition in general; but from the age of fifteen 'astrology was the main string to his plait of thought'. After burning too much midnight oil and neglecting his health, he suffered a nervous breakdown at twenty-one.

Old must have felt considerable relief upon finding a material toehold for all these ineffable preoccupations, when he moved to London early in 1889 and found himself in the thick of Theosophy — literally, since he and Blavatsky became very close and, when she moved to 19 Avenue Road, St John's Wood, in October 1889, he moved in too. This large and well-appointed house belonged to Annie Besant, Blavatsky's successor as leader of the T.S. Indeed, when H.P.B. died there, on 8 May 1891, Old was present — despite the fact that his own mother was also ill and died, rather uncannily, on the same day. His heart was never really in Theosophy after that and, five years later, he left the T.S. to pursue an insecure existence as a freelance writer. Writing as Sepharial, he produced three short-lived astrological magazines, countless articles and more than forty books. These included the obligatory textbook, *The Manual of Astrology*, which remained a standard text for the first three decades of the twentieth century. More frequent, however, were such works as *The Birthday Book of Destiny, The Great Devastation: A Prophecy of the Times that are Coming Upon Europe* and *Astrology for Beginners . . . Study Astrology! Forewarned is Forearmed*, the wartime reissue of his earlier *Elementary Astrology*. These provided his bread and butter and, from their profusion, it seems that Sepharial was continually on the verge of going without. One cannot avoid the impression that he was wasted on them, given the degree of learning and application that his articles in various specialist occult publications reflect; and he may well have felt so too.

Sepharial's views also came rather more down to earth. He quickly fastened on to Sir Oliver Lodge's recent observation that 'If once we grasp the idea that *past* and *future* may be *actually existing*, we can recognize that they may have a controlling influence on all present action.' But Sepharial had long maintained that astrology was founded on 'the imperishable rock of numbers' and should therefore be susceptible to precise verification. 'It is because of this mathematical basis,' he wrote, 'that the science is rendered so easy of proof, in contradistinction to many other less scientific modes of divination.' So, combining the necessity of commerce with the virtue of 'proof', Sepharial increasingly concentrated on devising complicated systems of astral forecasting for the stock-market and the turf, attracting both fans and detractors.

Undiscouraged by this mixed reception, Sepharial insisted that 'the gospel of true science is *utility*' and even that 'the sooner we bring the science [of astrology] down from the clouds where the would-be esotericists have incontinently harried it, the sooner will it gain a proper recognition in the practical world'. However, he died in Brighton on

23 December 1929 without ever seeing, or achieving for himself, such recognition. It might have consoled him to know that, nearly a century later, eleven of his books are still in print in Britain and America — a record many authors might envy.

Following Sepharial, Alan Leo joined Theosophical circles after moving to London in 1888. He took a small house at 12 Lugard Road in Peckham. At around this time, he also changed his name by deed poll to reflect his new life, as well as the preponderance of planets in that sign at his birth. In his daytime, 'exoteric' life, Leo was now the chief salesman for a confectionary firm. Reading through a shoe-string periodical called *The Astrologer*, he noticed a letter from F. W. Lacey (also known as 'Aphorel'), another astrologer living not far away in Brixton, and wrote to him.

Lacey turned out to be a kindred soul and fellow-Theosophist, whose own initiation into astrology was revealing. He had started off on Pearce's *Textbook of Astrology*, 'but not being a mathematician, I made very little progress'. He wrote to Sepharial 'and enquired whether he could recommend a simpler work . . . [He] advised me to start with Raphael's *Guide to Astrology*.' How many others were discouraged or defeated by Pearce's admirably but uncompromisingly stern and 'scientific' approach? Lacey and Leo, in this respect, were probably typical of most astrologers of the time.

The two decided that things should be easier for others like themselves and, equally important, that those others constituted an untapped market — a powerful combination. On 21 November 1889, after carefully noting the time, they decided to start a new astrological monthly periodical. Leo happened to mention the plan to Sepharial, who then quickly produced a rival, *Fate and Fortune*. Its first issue appeared in June 1890, one month before *The Astrologer's Magazine*. Sepharial's attempt failed after only four issues, however, confirming his remark that 'Left to myself, I would wreck the best business that was ever founded inside of twelve months.' In any event, it seems to have resulted in no ill will, and Leo and Lacey invited him to contribute to their own venture, which went from strength to strength and started to break even by June 1891.

Part of *The Astrologer's Magazine's* broad appeal can be judged from the clever choice of nativities to be discussed in the leading issue: those of Christ, taken from a seventeenth-century English astrologer; the Prince of Wales, the future Edward VII; and the African explorer Henry Stanley. Another reason for its success was probably the intemperate attacks made on it both by A. J. Pearce in *Zadkiel's Almanac*, and the *Daily News*. Most enticing of all, however, was the offer of a free horoscope for all new subscribers. These amounted to about 1,500 in the first year alone — a mixed blessing, since Leo and Lacey had to work flat out to provide even the brief delineations promised. By the end of 1891, Lacey felt obliged to resign, leaving Leo as the sole proprietor. Meanwhile, the latter somehow managed to carry on as a commercial traveller, combining his travels around the country with what is now sometimes called 'networking' with fellow Theosophists and astrologers. He also gave free lectures on the subject all over the country. In early 1891, for example, he lectured in Leamington, Liverpool, Burnley, Manchester, Bristol and Gloucester.

An unforeseen consequence of Leo's free offer was his own marriage. One of the circle of Theosophical astrologers that he had by now attracted, H. S. Green, interested a friend in the lodge in Bournemouth, who in turn convinced a fellow-member there to subscribe. Ada Elizabeth Murray Phillips, soon better known as Bessie Leo, was living in Southampton with her father. She was already well known locally as a palmist and phrenologist. In 1891, she read Sinnett's *Esoteric Buddhism* and, feeling just as many eclectic occultists of the time must have felt, upon encountering a capacious and comprehensive spiritual system that could accommodate them, immediately became, in her own words, 'an ardent Theosophist'.

In the winter of 1892, writing anonymously, Bessie sent off for her horoscope. The result so impressed her that she asked Green's friend to write to Leo, asking if he would consent to see her. In February 1893, in the course of one of his commercial peregrinations, he stopped off in Southampton one evening and called on his admirer. They 'at once plunged into occult and metaphysical subjects, until the hour of midnight had struck', he later recalled. In Bessie's words; 'We began to talk: Theosophy and astrology on his part, Phrenology and Palmistry on mine, for the latter two were my own studies; and time flew . . . I did not sleep much that night. It was all too wonderful. How I admired Mr. Leo's mind!'

But Bessie was already engaged to be married, on the understanding that the relationship was to be strictly platonic. In May, she and her husband moved to Bournemouth. Correspondence and occasional visits from Leo continued, in the course of which, he recollected, 'they sat conversing on very deep subjects, when the room became filled with a peculiar subtle influence enveloping them in a psychic aura which recurred on each meeting . . . it held them spellbound for about an hour.' Towards the end of 1894, Bessie's husband apparently tried to break the terms of their contract and the marriage was annulled the following spring. Bessie discussed remarriage with Alan, but she told him she feared that 'my father will never consent. You are a Christian, or at least a Theosophist, and he is a Jew, and very orthodox.' He replied,

> I am really an Astrologer and the Great Solar Logos and the star angels are my religion . . . If you decide to marry me, I will not let you work any more for money. You must give up your professional work, for I hold that a woman should be sheltered, protected and guarded within the home, and that she should leave the fight for maintenance and work to the man; then she has more power to develop her spiritual nature, and can help him to unfold his.

This was music to Bessie's ears, it seems, and as for the other little problem, marital celibacy, Alan had already declared his prior allegiance to the spiritual over the carnal life. I should add that he was neither hypocritical nor inconsistent in this vow. Within a few years, he had also become a vegetarian, teetotaller and non-smoker, all of which he remained until the end of his life. As Bessie put it: 'His ideal was purity, physical, mental and moral.'

So, on 23 September 1895, Bessie and Alan Leo married. It seems to have been a success for both partners. After Alan's death twenty-five years later, Bessie wrote rather touchingly: 'He was the sunshine of my life and home, he never once failed me in any event in life, and made me completely and entirely happy. Ours,' she added, 'was an astrological marriage, my Sun being on his Moon in the same degree of Aries.'

Celibacy for the purpose of transmuting sexual energy into spiritual was not rare among committed Theosophists, although more widely recommended than practised. It was part of a more general doctrine according to which, as Leo wrote, 'Woman is *not* woman, if she does not contain in her nature pure love, and man is not man who is not in his essence wisdom.' This view was apparently advocated with equal enthusiasm by many male and female Theosophists. It would strike a modern observer as confining women to a ghetto of nature and 'femaleness', leaving culture and initiative to men. At the time, however, it may have helped to create a valuable if temporary respite for women as recognized mistresses in their own and related spheres, at least. In any case, Alan frequently transgressed in practice, Bessie recalling that he 'was a great home lover and a real server in home life, quite as capable as a woman in the domestic sphere'.

Theosophy supplied people like Leo with a general social theory, embracing not only the question of sex but also that of class. Most important was the idea of one's karma, which accrued throughout different incarnations of the same soul and resulted in appropriate circumstances for the soul's growth at the next birth. 'I am convinced,' he wrote, 'that the problem of the inequalities of the human race can only be successfully solved by a knowledge of Astrology' — i.e. what he called esoteric astrology. The alternative, that one's circumstances were not 'earned', but random and arbitrary, was simply unacceptable: 'The law which gives to one soul a nativity of good environment in which refinement, opportunity, and sound moral training are uppermost; and to another poverty, disease, and immoral training, is manifestly unjust, to say the least, apart from its being without any apparent purpose.'

In this scheme of things, astrology supplied a symbolic key to the

individual's temperament (the prime circumstance for the present life),
and thereby both the traces of his or her past and the possibilities for
future development. All this was encoded in the nativity for the moment
of birth and needed only skilful interpretation to be laid bare . . . but
not by just anyone. As Leo came to see it, there were two schools of
astrology: 'The *esoteric* and the *fatalistic*'. The latter teaches that the
individual is

> the sport of an arbitrary power termed 'planet' . . . The former on the
> other hand, proclaims that 'character *and character alone*, determines
> destiny. It is not prediction, however accurate, that is needed at all, but
> what is needed is, the knowledge that each man is the law unto himself,
> that within each is the power to create his own destiny.'

Thus, for example, the first, fifth and ninth houses of a person's
nativity constitute, for Leo, 'the Mystic Triangle. Whoever can interpret
this can read the Past, the Present and the Future.' The eyes of the older
traditional astrology, however, would have perceived 'only' references
to one's physique, children and travels, respectively.

The marriage of natal astrology and Theosophy, therefore, seemed
not only provident but also necessary. Not surprisingly, Leo concluded:
'An astrologer must be first an occultist before he can become in any real
sense of the word an astrologer.' Everything conspired to facilitate this
consummation. As a theory, it explained Leo's own life-work, beginning
with the way he had immediately taken to the subject. 'I ought to know
something about Astrology,' he used to say modestly, 'for I believe I have
been an astrologer in several former lives.' Another problem it solved was
the fatalism of the old astral prophecy in an age that so valued individual
freedom and the ability to rise above one's circumstances. Even before
discovering Theosophy, Leo had found he 'could not reconcile the
fatalistic notions of materialistic Astrology with [my] own optimistic
views of free-will, and the value of individual effort'. Far from being
an irrational aberration, the new occult astrology was perfectly suited
to the capitalism and individualism of the age.

Finally, it also supplied an answer to one of the problems that most vexed late Victorians or, at least, those with sufficient leisure and inclination to feel so vexed. To adapt a more recent adage, it was as if they felt: 'Science — you can't live with it, you can't live without it.' In Leo's vision, however, 'Astrology — the "Wisdom of the Stars" — reveals a true Science, the beginning and the end of all scientific knowledge. In this sense Astrology is the philosophic link between Science and Religion.' This put science in its place and saved religion at a stroke, while ensuring a place for spiritual entrepreneurship. In short, he wrote: 'Although there is no system of thought more practical in matters concerning everyday life than Astrology, it is also the most transcendental study in the Universe.' What more could one want?

In 1895, shortly after their marriage, Alan and Bessie toured England, calling on other astrologers. Despite the fact that by now many if not most had allied themselves to his cause — A.J. Pearce being the leading exception — the results were disappointing. 'Some few astrologers there certainly were,' wrote Leo, 'who studied their science with reverence, but the majority paid more attention to the paper upon which their maps were drawn than to the Spiritual Intelligences connected with the planets.'

Already that year, *The Astrologer's Magazine* had also arrived at a crisis. During the five years of its existence, Leo and Lacey had sent out over 4,000 free horoscopes. Many of these resulted in requests for more detailed interpretations, combined with offers of payment. The result, as H. S. Green recalled, was 'so much additional work that eventually a small charge had to be made although there had originally been no intention to make the work professional, but it was practically unavoidable'. Beginning in 1893 with an anonymous request for a full reading accompanied by a £5 note, followed by a similar demand from the wife of a mayor in a provincial town (probably a fairly typical example of their constituency), Leo accepted money for anything more than the most basic horoscopic delineation. As we shall see, this proved to be a momentous decision. Even so, after five years, the amount of work involved showed no sign of diminishing and, despite the charges, the profits amounted, according to Leo, to the sum of £13! Understandably, he felt obliged to rethink things. And, as his tour confirmed, he had another reason for dissatisfaction: namely his inability, as yet, to convert enough astrologers to his vision of a truly spiritual science. In short, what he needed was a vehicle that was at once more popular, and therefore remunerative, *and* more Theosophical.

The result was the appearance, in late July of 1895, of *Modern Astrology*. 'The Editor,' it began, 'respectfully introduced this magazine to the intelligent portion of humanity' — a category, presumably, from which few would wish to exclude themselves — 'and particularly those for whom symbolical and metaphysical studies exercise a peculiar attraction. The time has come to modernise the ancient system of Astrology.'

Leo then opened another front. At noon on 14 January 1896, he founded the Astrological Society. Meeting at the magazine's new offices at 1–2 Bouverie Street, London E.C., the current Raphael, Robert T. Cross, agreed to act as vice-president and H. S. Green as treasurer, other officers were confirmed at the first annual general meeting. Meetings took place on the first Friday of every month and membership slowly grew to just over a hundred by the end of that year.

The new astrology, now fully and openly Theosophical, met with a mixed reaction. Some, especially among the Leos' extensive network of fellow-Theosophists, agreed with their friend Mrs Campbell Praed. She used, she said, to class astrology 'with *Fortune-telling*', but 'taught as Mr Leo taught it, Astrology now seems to me to be one of the best possible *guides to right living*'. However, there was plainly some resistance too, among astrologers used to a more down-to-earth approach. Bessie Leo, a frequent contributor to the new magazine, was obliged to note:

> In the pages of *Modern Astrology* articles have appeared, from time to time, containing what some of our readers term 'too much Theosophy'. It seems a curious fact that astrologers, and students of astrology, believers in the influence of the stars, should be orthodox. . . Yet again and again have readers expressed their opinion that there is too much 'Divine Wisdom' given out in the form of Astrology.

With characteristic bluntness, Bessie chastised such laggards for failing to appreciate 'a GREAT CENTRAL TRUTH'. 'Surely,' she wrote, '"practical" Astrology is the use of the science for *self-knowledge*, and the application if its wisdom to *self-unfoldment* . . . IT IS THE ATTITUDE OF MIND TOWARDS EVENTS THAT MATTERS, AND NOT THE EVENTS IN THEMSELVES.'

Be that as it may — and there is a lot to be said for Bessie's comments, if not necessarily for the way she expresses herself — Theosophical astrology continued to attract an increasing following of fairly well-educated, middle-class readers, especially but not only women, with a passionate interest in themselves and at least a general interest in astrology. The small community of professional astrologers became more divided than ever, however, and as the Leos' approach became increasingly more occultist and simultaneously popular, arousing suspicions of imperialism, so its hostility grew too. A. J. Pearce continued to fly the flag for a strictly scientific and mathematical astrology; Raphael resigned from the Astrological Society; and Sepharial too fell away, his disenchantment with the Theosophical Society growing after the death of his beloved Madame Blavatsky.

Alan and Bessie were undeterred. In 1898, they bought a terraced house, modest but adequate for their needs, at 9 Lyncroft Gardens in West Hampstead; and, towards the end of the year, aged thirty-eight, Alan Leo finally wound up his other commercial interests and turned to astrology full-time. This was a brave step, because serious problems remained. Since launching *Modern Astrology*, Leo had sunk almost £1,000 into it in four years. It was only beginning to attract sufficient subscribers to cover its expenses. As he knew from his experience with the earlier offer of free horoscopes, something similar would prove a good, even crucial draw. But how to exploit it without being overwhelmed by the sheer volume of work? Leo already employed someone to do the mathematical calculations and others to write down his judgements while he dictated, but, as he recalled, 'even then I was a slave, bound hand and foot'. Finally, illness from exhaustion obliged him once again to reconsider his entire *modus operandi*. Writing in 1903, he decided:

... the horoscopes were *too long*. In fact, I was giving too much for the money. So I made arrangements with my clerk to stop me when a certain number of lines were written, according to the amount paid for the delineation.

Mr Strutton (who was then my chief clerk) is no longer in my employ, but to him belongs the credit of inventing an ingenious scheme for regulating the flow of my eloquence. He let me run on for just so many pages under each heading, and took carbon copies for reference. One day he pointed out, to my astonishment, the fact that in all cases when treating of the same rising sign, or lunar position, etc., there was a similarity in style and matter — the sheets were in fact virtual *facsimiles* ... Several hundred of these carbon copies were collected, and the idea then occurred to me to have them arranged, and the essence of each separate page specially typed and then mimeographed.

What Leo realized was that in response to a request for a horoscope he, or rather his employees, could simply staple together and send off the relevant mimeographed sheets for the Sun's sign, the Moon's, the ascendant and its ruling planet, and so on — the higher the price, the more detail and therefore the greater number of sheets. Furthermore, this method solved the age-old problem of an unknown birth-time. Leo 'was daily writing to say that I could not give a horoscope without the time of birth, but almost invariably the reply came back: "Please try your best for me, I want you to help me if you can."' Now any sheets containing information depending on a time were simply omitted and a note attached saying that the delineation was the best that could be provided.

Having left Bouverie Street in 1900 (the building was torn down for redevelopment) and returned to work at Lyncroft Gardens, Leo fitted out his study with lockers containing nearly a hundred 'Stone Patent Drawer Boxes', each with its pile of delineation-sheets, and the production-line was ready. Thus was born the first modern astrological business. The boxes have been replaced by computers and the analyses are now 'interactive' rather than simply additive, but the basic model has not changed a bit.

Then,

> One day, while calmly thinking the matter over, a suggestion was dropped into my mind by some kind intelligence to try the public with a 1 shilling 'test' horoscope . . . My first advertisement appeared in *Light*, and the Test Horoscopes quickly 'caught on'. I then extended the advertisement to the monthly journals, for I now saw a means of introducing the science to many who had never heard of Astrology before. The result was that upwards of 20,000 test horoscopes were sent out in three years, each advertisement offering to return money if the horoscope was not true.

The test horoscopes for one shilling not only led indirectly to more subscriptions to *Modern Astrology*, they also brought in orders for more detailed readings for five guineas each and more, all the way up to twenty-five pounds. For the first time, financial security, 'four figures a year', was in sight. Did the Leos celebrate in style and move into something bigger?

Hardly; most of the profits were ploughed straight back into publishing a series of books, seven in all, and cheaper pocket manuals. Leo's aim is clear enough from their titles. The series and its first volume, appearing in 1901, were entitled *Astrology for All*. They were priced at twelve shillings and sixpence each, and together constituted a fairly complete if oversimplified means whereby someone could learn to draw up and interpret a nativity. And, painlessly enough, 'The first map a student should study will be his own.' Introducing the project, Leo declared defiantly: 'The day is past for writing a defense of Astrology . . . The best test that can be applied, to this as to all other subjects where first-hand knowledge is required, is that of experience.'

The pocket manuals, beginning with *Everybody's Astrology*, sold for one shilling and eightpence each. Most such guides were pitched at the most elementary level possible — for example, from *Astrology*

Explained:

    1 *What is Astrology?* A knowledge of the Stars.
    2 *How may we obtain that knowledge?* Through an open mind and
    ordinary study.
    3 *What are the Stars?* The Mansions of Spiritual Intelligences.*
    (* 'In my Father's house are many mansions.' John. xiv, 2.)

This was Leo at his most populist, aiming to put astrology into the
hands of as many people as humanly possible, who could then act as
their own astral interpreters.

The following year, with this project under way, Leo abruptly resigned
from the presidency of the Astrological Society, which without his driving
force quickly collapsed. Then, on the evening of 5 December 1902, in a
meeting at 28 Albermarle Street, the Society for Astrological Research
came into being. The council included Bessie, Green, Sepharial and
Bailey, the sub-editor of *Modern Astrology*; Pearce had been invited,
but wrote to say that he could 'only unite with those who followed
the Placidean method of *Primary Directions*'. Within less than a year,
however, Leo had decided to withdraw from this organization too,
explaining to his readers:

> I have failed in my attempt to bring together those whom I had hoped
> were strong enough to place truth and their love of Astrology before petty
> personal bias, and narrow-minded adherence to exclusive 'systems', and I
> am not at all sure that the new Society for Astrological Research will prove
> a sufficiently advanced body in which to form the nucleus of an Esoteric
> School of Modern Astrologers.

Another crisis now blew up. Leo employed nine people, excluding
Bessie, in his astrological cottage industry at Lyncroft Gardens. Sensitive
to charges of crass commercialism, they had been growing increasingly
restless about his mass-marketing methods and, very possible, the
work-load. Finally, in 1903, there was a walk-out led by Bailey.
He issued his own more traditionalist magazine, *Destiny*, the following year, in which there appeared the portrait of Leo at work

quoted at the beginning of this chapter. Bailey continued to be highly critical of Leo. In 1907, he started an upmarket version of *Old Moore's*, which in 1914 evolved into *The British Journal of Astrology*. Sepharial, equally disaffected, became a principal contributor to both titles, which maintained high standards until the *Journal*'s demise in 1939.

Bailey's other project, a British College of Astrology, ultimately came to nothing, but he continued to represent a particular kind of astrologer — waspish, obsessed with mathematical and empirical precision, alternately self-important and craving wider recognition — who always seems to pop up somewhere. In 1919, he is described giving a public lecture on the degenerative influence of Neptune:

> instancing Cubists and Futurists in art, syncopated music, Jazz bands, and various American dances, which he ascribed as due to Neptune, and which were lowering the standard of both art and music. He also spoke in very strong terms of the Neptunian idea of Democracy, which, he stated, was a wild, mad delusion, of wild, mad men and women ... who were turning the world upside down by their utopian and inverted ideas of liberty and equality.

Not much spirit of the Aquarian Age there! And rather more, albeit with hindsight, of the early fascism of the 1920s.

The collapse of the society and the walk-out proved but temporary setbacks to Leo. Other helpers, inspired or charmed by his charisma and loyal to Theosophical ideals, quickly replaced the disaffected. The ranks of followers continued to grow, with or without a formal body, and the books rolled out — *The Horoscope and How to Read it* and *Practical Astrology* in 1902, *How to Judge a Nativity and Theoretical Astrology* by H. S. Green in 1903, *Casting the Horoscope* and a new edition of *Astrology for All* in 1904. In January 1909, *Modern Astrology* and Leo's horoscopic production-line returned to the City of London, taking offices at 42–3 and 50 Imperial Buildings, Ludgate Circus. On 24 April, seventy-five people attended a meeting he called to initiate yet another organization, the Astrological Society, and the second by that name; meeting weekly, it soon attracted about 200 members.

We get some idea of what Leo promised his members from his address to the first annual general meeting of the Astrological Society held at the Food Reform Restaurant on Furnival Street, E.C., on 28 May of the following year. Leo here speaks in a rather more unbuttoned way than he usually permitted himself to write:

> I do not think anyone in this room realises what a power one gets the moment one realises what pure Astrology is. It is undoubtedly one of the great occult forces in the world, because you know exactly the time when great things are operating in the world, and if you knew a little more you would know just how to act at those times.
>
> ... The first and most essential thing for every Astrologer is that he should live a pure life ... I know for a positive fact that there are great Beings connected with Astrology with whom you have only to come into touch for whole worlds to be unsealed, and whose influence is so mighty and vast as to be quite impossible to put into words, and you can quite see that unless you have a pure magnetism yourself, what an enormous power you have for harm.

In June 1909, the Leos found themselves in the probate and divorce courts, sitting before Sir John Bigham and a special jury. Bessie's father had died on 8 March 1908 and his will, which he had only recently made out, named Bessie as his sole heir and left her in possession of his property, valued at about £80,000, a considerable sum. Some distant relatives decided to contest this will, asserting that he had been unduly and deliberately influenced by the Leos, who were 'adventurers in Spiritualism, Palmistry and Astrology'. This was the basis of the relatives' case and their solicitor hammered away at the point, describing the Leos — in terms unchanged since Zadkiel's trial nearly fifty years earlier — as 'the greatest possible humbugs, making their living by the rankest kind of imposture'. Bessie's counsel, however, insisted that the only question to decide was whether her father was of sound mind when the will was executed; and the evidence showed that he had been. In his summing-up, the judge, as we might expect, severely castigated astrology, but advised a narrow interpretation of the legal question at hand. The jury found for Bessie.

It was a favourable verdict, then, but an unpleasant experience none the less, and one which opened Leo's eyes. 'In regard to the insinuations of the plaintiff's Counsel,' he wrote afterwards, 'and the apparent bias and prejudice of the Judge, I must confess my amazement. It seems to me manifestly unfair . . . ' However knowledgeable about the spiritual and even business worlds he may have been, Leo was still remarkably naïve about the world of social and cultural power. And of history; was he unaware, for example, of the prosecution of R. H. Penny?

Penny contributed occasional astrological items to *St Stephen's Review, The Tribune, Society, The Review of Reviews* and *Borderland*, to whose readers he appeared as 'Neptune'. He was a close friend of W. T. Stead, the adventurous and open-minded editor of *The Pall Mall Gazette*. In 1886, he was entrapped by a police 'client' and successfully prosecuted at Bow Street for fortune-telling. He received twenty-one days' imprisonment and a five-pound fine. His appeal, heard the following year, was rejected. Neither Penny's many character-references nor his impeccable naval background provided any defence; nor did the representations of C. C. Massey, an articulate member of a distinguished political family and first president of the British Theosophical Society, who acted as his solicitor. Indeed, the judge at the appeal, Justice Denman, remarked that it was 'incredible that any sane person in the present age could conceivably believe in astrology'. To add to the incongruity, which he evidently relished, Penny was later picked to be among the veterans presented to the queen at Windsor on 16 May 1898.

Thus, when Alan and Bessie left London on 12 November 1909 for India, it was perhaps as much for an unwonted holiday after the trial as for spiritual enlightenment. They joined Annie Besant, now president of the T.S., in Madras. In between seeing the sights and comparing notes with Indian astrologers, Leo found time to ponder upon something from home. It was the matter of the Test Horo-scopes.

This problem was a consequence of their success. By now they had spawned dozens of imitators. Seven were described in an article in the journal *Truth* on 13 April 1910, entitled 'Star-Readers and Moon Calves', four of whom worked London's West End: 'Madame Chester' (63 Bessborough Place); 'Old Sol' (155 High Street Kensington); 'Pro-fessor Zazra' (90 New Bond Street); and the felicitously named 'Newton Verity' (4 Duke Street). Responding to their notices in various monthly magazines (six out of the seven advertised in *The Woman at Home*), the writer sent in his birth-data along with a one-shilling postal order and two penny stamps. In return, he received sketches of the barest, vaguest and most flattering nature, including some rather contradictory information on his lucky stone (ranging from turquoise to diamonds and opals), colour (covering the entire spectrum) and day (Thursday or Friday), along with invitations to send larger amounts for more of the same: five shillings to Madame Chester for '"a larger and more carefully calculated horoscope", together with "a moon-table for daily use"'; and Old Sol 'as a very special favour will give you a "daily guide horoscope" for half his usual fee of 15s.' Newton Verity, the writer continued, 'has a very complete thing for a guinea, and Zazra has a speciality, highly recommended, at the reduced figure of 15s., and if you do not care to invest that amount he will sell you a Crystal Gazing Outfit for half a crown by which you can read the future for yourself, or an Indian Fakir Mirror as used by Jadoo Wallah of Hindoostan'.

The *Truth*'s report attracted much comment from other newspapers, including the complaint about 'a confusion of prophets'. The writer noted chivalrously that woman 'is far more amenable to suggestions of occult or pseudo-occult lore than the mere male, and there is a very real danger that she may be led to waste her money on the idiotic advice and warnings of the star-readers. Hence the need for protecting her against the insidious wiles of the fortune-teller . . . ' He concluded, ominously:

I wonder that the law on the subject is not more frequently enforced. If a gipsy woman is caught bamboozling a servant girl at a back door she is hauled before the magistrates and sent to prison without the option of a fine, but the fortune-teller who has sufficient capital to insert an advertisement in a newspaper or magazine . . . is allowed to carry on business without let or hindrance. The law holds that both the gipsy and the advertising astrologer who purports to read the future are equally 'rogues and vagabonds', and there is no reason why if one is punished the other should be allowed to go scot free.

This article was placed before Leo upon his return to London on 21 April. He had already been aware of the problem before his departure, but it must have made very uncomfortable reading, particularly since all these artists called themselves astrologers, and used 'a circular taken from a stock of common forms', in other words, precisely the system he had pioneered. In the next issue of *Modern Astrology*, he announced the end of the test horoscopes. Already, while abroad, he had written, 'I had the opportunity of seeing several of the "test horoscopes" that were being sent out by so-called "professors", the majority of whom it was quite evident had no actual knowledge of Astrology, but were mere imitators of our methods.' Owing to this abuse, therefore, 'from now onward this method of advertising will be abandoned, and propaganda work, if continued, will take another form'.

Leo was unapologetic: 'The purpose and intention of the Test Horoscope was to prove to the casual but sceptical "outsider" that there really was "something in Astrology". Having done this, it has served its purpose.' But he was bluffing. Despite their success, the horoscopes had failed to remedy what was arguably the root problem, namely the view of astrology as fortune-telling. For that reason, he admitted, 'I am reluctantly continuing the professional work I had hoped to discontinue about this time, and until the general public are educated into a better knowledge of what Astrology really is, I shall continue to judge horoscopes and write books on the subject.' Thus did Leo, aged fifty, sense that despite his desire to move on and 'further the cause from a much higher altitude', he was becoming yet more firmly nailed to the cross of his cause. Meanwhile, in response to the newspaper revelations, a storm was brewing in other kinds of high circles in London. A keen ear could have detected the sound of copies of the Vagrancy Act being brought down from an upper shelf and the dust being blown off.

Of that, Leo was still oblivious. His involvement with Theosophy continued to deepen; as he had written in *Modern Astrology* a few years earlier: 'I must admit that I have been swinging very much in the direction of the esoteric side of the science, for, to speak candidly, it is the only part of the science that really interests me.' In the early spring of 1911, he and Bessie travelled a second time to India.

Meanwhile, the Theosophical Society was at a fever pitch of excitement. Madame Blavatsky had once intimated that its real purpose was to prepare the world for the reappearance of the Lord Maitreya, otherwise known as the 'World Teacher', whose last public tenancy had been the body of Jesus. His arrival would coincide with that of a new 'sub-race' in human evolution — the sixth sub-race of the fifth root-race, to be precise — probably in California. (The smart money is still on Marin County.) This idea was enthusiastically adopted, although the timetable was somewhat speeded up, by Annie Besant. And sure enough, early in 1909, her colleague and occult mentor, C. W. Leadbeater, clairvoyantly discovered the long-awaited 'vehicle' in the person of a handsome fourteen-year-old Indian boy, Jiddu Krishnamurti.

On 5 May 1911, shepherded by Annie Besant and a bevy of devotees, including Alan and Bessie, Krishnamurti arrived on his first trip to England. They were met at Charing Cross Station by a large and emotional contingent of Engish Theosophists. Among them was Emily, Lady Lutyens, wife of the architect Edwin Lutyens and granddaughter of the late but still ubiquitous Sir Edward Bulwer-Lytton, whom Leadbetter had already declared, on the strength of *Zanoni*, to have been an initiate. In the next few days, she became the national representative of the new organization centred on Krishnamurti, the Order of the Star in the East. The Leos were in the first rush to join. Sepharial was not, bitterly remarking: 'It says very little for the inspired actions of the Theosophical leaders that they should choose the very lamest of lame ducks to represent for them the *avatar* (Messiah) of a new spiritual movement.'

This was the heady milieu in which Alan and Bessie lived and moved during these years. Pausing only to beget his fourth organization in 1912 — the Astrological Institute, for professional astrologers — Alan Leo continued his occult studies. The following year, the seventh and final volume of the *Astrology for All* series was published: *Esoteric Astrology*. By now, the thread connecting Leo's populism and occultism in his over-all programme had at last snapped, leaving the former stranded. The book was intended to be his final testament to the integration of Western astrology and Eastern philosophy, but with its welter of auras, etheric doubles and a seemingly arbitrary re-ordering of traditional astrological significations, *Esoteric Astrology* was later described by one of his most loyal adherents, Charles Carter, as 'Leo's least satisfactory work . . . a big volume containing virtually nothing worth reading'.

The long-intended blow finally fell on the afternoon of 29 April 1914. Two men called on Leo as he was working in the *Modern Astrology* offices in Imperial Buildings. They were shown in and one of them handed him a piece of paper, which read:

> INFORMATION has been laid this day by Hugh McLean of the City of London Police for THAT YOU, on the twenty-seventh day of February, 1914 in the said City of London did UNLAWFULLY PRETEND TO TELL FORTUNES to DECEIVE and IMPOSE upon the said Hugh McLean and others of His Majesty's subjects contrary to the Statute.

Leo was summoned, in conclusion, to appear at the police courts, Mansion House, on Wednesday, 6 May at 11.15 a.m. The order was signed by Sir T. Vansittart Bowater, the lord mayor.

The first thing Leo did (and if a test is ever required to detect hidden astrologers, this one would do) was to glance at his watch to note the time. The second was to exclaim, 'This, after twenty-five years! Who is Hugh McLean?' 'I am,' the detective present answered. 'I have not told your fortune,' Leo replied. 'I have never seen you before, and I do not tell fortunes.' Then, after bidding them good day and showing them out, he asked one of his assistants to make out a horoscope for 4.15 p.m. and returned to finish his work.

Upon returning home that evening, Leo considered the resulting map. He decided that it boded well and left him in a strong position. After discussing the matter with Bessie and the next morning calling on his solicitor, who took a gloomy view, Leo engaged a legal firm and asked Mr W. R. Warren to appear as his counsel. He gave instructions that, if he was convicted, his case should be taken to a higher court and a final appeal, 'in order that the distinction between Astrology and fortune-telling could be definitely decided'.

The court-room, now unused, at Mansion House was small and austere. The accused was led up some stairs and through a hatch-door to sit on a wooden chair behind an iron railing, looking up at the judge. Apart from counsel and clerks, there was space on either side for a few witnesses and members of the public. On the day of the hearing, the lord mayor — not, apparently, a happy man — was sitting and Mr Vickery, the assistant city solicitor, prosecuting. Leo pleaded not guilty. Annie Besant, A. P. Sinnett and Sepharial attended to speak on his behalf and reporters were there from *The Times*, the *Star*, the *Globe*, the *Evening News* and the *Evening Standard*, as well as from *The Occult Review*.

The hearing opened at 11.15 a.m. sharp. After the charge had been read, Mr Vickery opened the case for the prosecution by saying that the defendant carried on the business of fortune-telling in 'an open and flagrant way' at Imperial Buildings, Ludgate Circus. Detective-inspector McLean had written to him in February asking for a list of horoscopes and their prices. He received in reply a booklet entitled *The Stars and How to Read Them*, which listed charges from five shillings to five guineas, the latter for a ten-year look-out. Using the name of William Hammond, McLean wrote back asking for the complete horoscope for ten shillings, giving his birth-data as 6 a.m., 22 February 1875, at Ryde on the Isle of Wight.

In return, he received a 'Delineation of Nativity', with a covering letter, which was read aloud in court. It began thus: 'This abridged delineation is only a brief sketch of your nativity, but it may be considerably enlarged either by purchasing a special and complete judgement or by judging it yourself from *The Key to Your Nativity*.' The witness said that, among other things, he was advised 'to avoid accidents and to keep his blood pure'. (Some laughter in the court at this.) One section was entitled 'Future Prospects' and addressed the next five years in the life of the subject. A forecast that in 1914 the inspector would 'come into contact with peculiar strangers' would be hard to deny. Not surprisingly, Mr Vickery passed over the character analysis to emphasize this kind of prognostication. Mr Warren, however, denied that any fortune-telling had taken place. After pointing out that at the time the letter had been written and sent Leo had in fact been abroad, he proceeded to cross-examine Inspector McLean. Did he know that Mr Leo had been casting horoscopes for twenty-five years and had written many books on the subject? At which the lord mayor remarked: 'I do not care if a thousand books have been written, I have no doubt that there has been an endeavour to tell fortunes.' Was the inspector aware, then, that Mr Leo had received testimonials from some 20,000 persons, some of them holding the highest positions in this country? Mr Warren then elicited the fact that the inspector had not only used an assumed name but had also invented his birth-data. Here the lord mayor again interrupted Mr Warren to say: 'What you are trying to prove is that if the Inspector had given the right date you would have been able to tell what was going to happen in the future.' To which Mr Warren replied: 'I am not saying so, and the book does not say so.'

Then, before either Leo or any of his witnesses had been called to the stand, the lord mayor announced: 'I cannot see that this letter of February 27th has been proved, and so I shall dismiss that summons.' He refused Mr Warren's request for costs. Regarding a second summons, for a similar offence in April, Mr Warren again argued that the defendant had no case to answer, since there was no evidence that he had had any knowledge of either the inspector's application or the horoscope sent in response. The lord mayor responded: 'On that technical objection, I feel I am bound to dismiss this summons. At the same time,' he added, 'I am fully convinced in my own mind that there is no doubt that this is endeavouring to tell fortunes.' There was applause in the court, but costs were again refused.

Thus, after about two hours, both summonses were dismissed on technical grounds, which left everyone unsatisfied: the prosecution, for obvious reasons, but also the astrologers. One astrologer was even unhappy for the same reason as the prosecution. Showing on a minuscule scale how dogmatic rivals often prefer the common enemy to win, Leo's ex-employee, Bailey concluded sternly that 'the majority of the prosecutions have been, some wholly and others in part, quite justified, and secondly, that those who have been prosecuted have only themselves to blame'. Sepharial rallied round, however, asking in *Modern Astrology* how it was possible to class 'a tax-payer, a payer of Education and Poor Rates, a house-holder, and . . . a reputable publisher of numerous works in every sense educative with the other objects of the Vagrancy Act such as "keepers of houses of ill-fame", "poultry thieves", "itinerant fortune-tellers" and "vagrants".'

According to an astrologer from Sheffield, George Wilde, the whole thing had resulted from 'public opinion, fed by the Press exposures of the West End horde of dubious foreigners':

Incalculable mischief was done by some American astrologers (who knew little about the art and less about the science) arriving here hoping to reap a rich harvest. They made no calculations, but merely looked into the almanac to see which sign the sun was in; then after giving a stereotyped reading from that they actually copied the birthday information from almanacs and sent the same predictions to a thousand people born on the same day, but in different years. That this was deception cannot be denied. And so the victims realized the humbug of it all, when they compared their readings. The Home Secretary took the opinion of the Law Officers of the Crown, and they are the authorities who have instructed the Commissioner of Police to take proceedings.

Wilde's account may not have needed the addition of interfering foreigners to be effective, but it rings true. The police had indeed been instructed to act, and as the country's most visible if not eminent astrologer, Leo — whose test horoscopes were the inspiration to this flock of illegitimate imitators — was the obvious choice of target.

No one was more dissatisfied with the verdict than Leo himself. 'I had resolved to retire from professional work next year,' he wrote in *Modern Astrology*. 'I have now however no intention of retiring until I have done my best to free the science of Astrology from the taint of common fortune-telling, and I hope this will be accomplished within the next three years.'

Immediately after the trial, Leo supplied his barrister with copies of everything he had published and a full range of typical horoscopes, asking him for a legal opinion. Mr Warren had replied, in part, that without expressing any opinion on the subject of Leo's works he would be ready to contend that the aims of his books were 'far higher than and widely different from fortune-telling or mere peeps into the future. And if ever Mr Alan Leo should be attacked on the ground of his PRINTED WORKS I am of the opinion that he would have an incontrovertible answer to any such charge.'

As Leo knew, however, that was not enough. The problem lay with the horoscopes he supplied, since in a climate of disbelief in occult means of discerning the future, even in broad outline, any such prediction whatsoever — whether based on a card trick or pages of mathematical calculations — must inevitably count as fortune-telling. Therefore, he resolved:

> Let us part company with the fatalistic astrologer who prides himself on his predictions and who is ever seeking to convince the world that in the predictive side of Astrology alone shall we find its value. We need not argue the point as to its reality, but instead make a much-needed change in the meaning of the word and call Astrology the science of *tendencies*, thus

giving a more elastic interpretation of the old but very good astrological word 'influence'.

This position had the advantage of bringing astrology into line with the general position of the discipline of psychology, which, even without legal pressure, was finding it equally necessary to allow for human beings' stubborn insusceptibility to precise 'scientific prediction'. In fact, Leo was arguably in advance of academic psychology here; suffering from a bad case of physics envy, it was still resisting any such realism by either concentrating on more manageable trivia (physiological reaction times etc.) or fixing tight and highly artificial experimental parameters.

Leo already disliked astral prediction anyway, having identified it with the materialistic and deterministic old astrology which he was trying to replace. *The Key to Your Own Nativity*, the very book which the first letter to 'William Hammond' had recommended, stated that 'the horoscope shows influences at work, be the subject peer or peasant; but to the peer honour means the purple, to the peasant at best but the parish council. The horoscope is written in a symbology that speaks of *principles*, not particulars . . . ' Unfortunately, as Leo once complained:

> friends, clients, and those interested, are not satisfied with character delineations, and invariably we heard the exclamation: 'Oh, yes, I know all about my character, but what I want to know is my future' . . . To satisfy this demand the astrological student begins to dabble in forecasting, and he is fortunate if he remembers that CHARACTER IS DESTINY and keeps the radix or nativity before him.

But to the extent that Leo actually carried out his promise to eliminate prediction, the appeal of his popular revolution was bound to encounter its limits.

Sometime around 1914, Alan and Bessie left Lyncroft Gardens for 'Dollis Lodge', a much larger detached house, built in mock-Tudor style, on Dollis Avenue in the northern suburb of Finchley, London. It is still the sort of street where the houses have names instead of numbers.

On the evening of 13 July 1914, they held an informal meeting to which about seventeen other people were invited. After refreshments in the garden, the gathering withdrew to the Leos' drawing-room and, at about 7.15 p.m. Alan spoke, saying that it seemed to him and Bessie that the time was ripe for the amalgamation of Theosophy and astrology in a new lodge of the Theosophical Society. Those present were therefore offered the privilege of being its founding members. Bessie was to be its president and he the vice-president; meetings would be held every Monday evening at 2 Upper Woburn Place. Bessie spoke briefly of her pleasure in being the mother to this new enterprise, founded to 'teach Astrology to Theosophists and Theosophy to Astrologers'. After a little discussion, the proposal was unanimously agreed.

Among those present was a young solicitor, Charles E. O. Carter, who displaced Bessie seven years later as president of the Middlesex Lodge, or the Astrological Lodge of the Theosophical Society, as it became four months later. Carter held that position for thirty years. Writing many years later, after the death of both Bessie and Alan, he recalled: 'Properly speaking, our Lodge was founded at his instigation, by Mrs Leo.' At the time, Alan was reported to have confided that he had 'set it in motion to give Mrs Leo something to occupy herself with'. Carter portrays Bessie in a rather unflattering light: 'She was possessed by an itch for power but she was totally incompetent and very indolent. This led to an attitude of constant ineffectual interference.'

Things got off to a good start. At the first meeting on 13 September, A. P. Sinnett was the honoured guest. Speaking informally, he stressed the importance of astrology and hinted that he had 'evidence that the Masters themselves base prediction for the future on astrological conditions'. Lady Lutyens was a guest speaker a couple of months later, addressing the lodge on 'The Coming of the World Teacher', i.e. Krishnamurti.

In addition to his membership of various Masonic lodges, this was actually the fourth Theosophical lodge Alan, together with Bessie, had created. As Carter remarks, he also 'had' an astrological society and a professional institute, *Modern Astrology* and a thriving professional practice. 'He certainly does not appear to have had any inkling that, of all his work, only the [Astrological] Lodge would survive his death for any considerable time.' Even that was in doubt for a while, as after Leo's death dissatisfaction with Bessie's heavy-handed Theosophy grew steadily and membership dwindled to about thirty. Finally, Bessie was ousted as president in 1922. The fact was, as Carter put it, 'people came to an astrological lodge to hear astrology, and that is what we gave them'. With its weekly Monday evening meetings and quarterly periodical, the lodge hung on and its membership slowly grew again. Other groups split off, for the most part amicably: the overtly non-Theosophical, and soon larger Astrological Association; a teaching body, the Faculty of Astrological Studies; and most recently the Company of Astrologers — in other words, almost every major English astrological organization.

But Alan Leo's trials were not yet over. The issue of *Modern Astrology* for September 1917 was headlined 'REX v. LEO' and began: 'A "bomb" more cruel than the German air raiders' bomb fell into the astrological camp on July 2nd, when we were served with a summons to appear at the Mansion House at 11.30 a.m. on July 9th on a charge of "pretending and professing to tell fortunes".'

Evidently, the public prosecutor had decided, or been instructed, to bring back a prosecution. This must have been a real blow for Leo. Aged fifty-seven, his 'three years to clear Astrology from the taint of common fortune-telling' were almost over; but he was no nearer even retiring to write full-time, let alone achieving that greater goal.

At the request of his counsel, still Mr Warren, Leo wrote off to ask for help, especially letters of character-reference, to be sent c/o Warren's clerk, Mr Attenborough. Among the replies came this one, dated 4 July, from Shute End Lodge, Wokingham:

Dear Mr Leo, I am so sorry to hear these Jupiterians are at it again —
when will they learn sense? If you want an influential witness why not try
Baillie Weaver, Lady de la Warr and Miss de Normann? As directors of the
Theosophical Educational Trust they are supporters of astrology in schools,
and can testify that the children's horoscopes are invaluable. Baillie Weaver
is a lawyer himself, and with his aristocratic and penguin-like manner will
appeal to the other penguins at the Mansion House. Graham Pole and his
brother are also directors of the Trust. — Wishing you a triumphal scoring
off silly Jupiterians — Yours sincerely, Ch. M. Adam.

More typical and revealing, if less apt, was that of William Learoyd, writing on the following day from Chester: 'I am quite unable to suggest the
name of any influential people who would openly venture to support you
in this. You know how many upon whom the claims of astrology have
compelled acceptance shrink from this fact being publicly or generally
known.' As if to underline the point, C. Audrey wrote on the 9th: 'I did
not see my way to give help exactly in the way suggested in your letter
— but I gave help by giving spiritual assistance which you personally
deserve and I feel sure you will be protected and no harm will come to
you.' And although E. M. Machattie, upon receiving Leo's letter on 7
July, 'hastened to town early to ask leave from my principals to attend
Mr Attenborough's office ... Much to my distress and concern they
expressed a wish that I would not act in the matter at all — even in
so far as writing to Mr Attenborough.'

The trial opened on 9 July, once again at Mansion House. As before,
reporters from several newspapers were present, including *The Times*,
the *Daily News* and the *Star*; and the witnesses for Leo, who once more
pleaded not guilty, again included A. P. Sinnett, now aged seventy-five.
The judge was Mr Alderman Moore. Mr Travers Humphreys, acting on
behalf of the Director of Public Prosecutions, said that the defendant
advertised horoscopes 'and things of that sort'. Inspector Nicholls of the
city police had sent in five guineas, and obtained in return a document
of about 25,000 words in length which contained predictions for the
next ten years. 'A great deal of this,' he said, 'was unintelligible jargon,

but upon specific passages the present proceedings were instigated.' He then read several such passages out, including at least one specific and personal prediction, namely that 'at this time a death in your family circle is likely to cause you sorrow'. In short, it was 'preposterous that persons for the sake of money should be allowed to make a living by professing to be able to predict the future'. The defendant may even be sincere, but to quote Mr Justice Denman, dismissing R. H. Penny's appeal in 1887, where something was asserted that was so ridiculous that 'no sane man could possibly believe it', then it was not necessary to prove intent to deceive.

Mr Wild, for the defence, said he was basing his client's case upon two propositions. Firstly, the defendant had had no intention to deceive or impose which, he argued, must be the case for a conviction. Astrology was believed in by millions of people, including many of learning and renown — Dr Richard Garnett, the late Keeper of Printed Books at the British Museum, for example. (Garnett would not have appreciated being cited in this context, but he was no longer able to object.) His client was thus practising a science in which he had a bona fide belief. He was the author of seven large works and fourteen smaller manuals on the subject, and he, Mr Wild, would bring forward evidence to show not only the high character of the defendant, but the value of the astrological advice he had given in the past. As for Mr Justice Denman's point, in 1887 'no sane man' would have believed in ever seeing the bones of one's hand by Röntgen rays, or that an enemy could have dropped bombs on London from flying machines! Who knows whether the next thirty years might not bring a general recognition of astrology?

At about this point in Mr Wild's address, he was obliged to break off for the rising of the court. Adjourned for a week, the case resumed on 16 July. Mr Wild now turned to his second proposition: his client did not tell fortunes. That involved predicting future events, whereas Mr Leo merely discussed tendencies. Indeed, Mr Leo not only did not claim to predict the future but also declared himself unable to do so, since — in accordance with the ancient dictum, 'The stars incline, they do not compel' — free-will was integral to astrology. The Sun in astrology, Mr

Wild continued, waxing lyrical, really represented a great onmipotent intelligence, whose outposts were the encircling planetary angels — the fingers, as it were, of one great hand.

This time, Leo was called to the witness stand. He affirmed that he did not claim to be able to predict the future and agreed that his personal clients were mainly among 'the rich and intellectual classes'. Confirming his belief in the truth of astrology, he added: 'I most emphatically say that I do not tell fortunes. I tell *tendencies* from the horoscope, and in every horoscope I send out I make that statement.' When Leo was cross-examined on this point, and in particular on the technical basis for the predictions in question, he asked Mr Humphreys; 'Do you wish me to explain Astrology to you?' To which the latter replied; 'God forbid!' Mr Humphreys concentrated his fire rather on the defence of 'tendencies', asking Leo sarcastically; 'Is this death a tendency, or is there a tendency to be dead?'

Leo's loyal sub-editor Alfred Barley, sitting in the court, later felt that in the end, 'the whole case had hinged round this point'. Neither Leo's bona fides nor his sincerity had been questioned; indeed, at one point the judge said that he was quite prepared to admit that astrology was a science that was studied by a great many people. But against the charge of predicting the future, i.e. 'fortune-telling', the defence of 'tendencies' proved, as Barley wrote, 'but a broken reed', being portrayed as 'a mere "get-out"'. Given the unfortunate example of a 'death in the family' showcased by the prosecution, it is not hard to see why. Despite his unusually disinterested, even sympathetic attitude, which softened the blow somewhat, Mr Alderman Moore evidently agreed. This was his judgement:

> After a very patient hearing of the able and ingenious arguments of Mr Wild, the defendant's counsel, and evidence for the accused, I find the defendant did unlawfully pretend and profess to tell fortunes, contrary to the form of the Statute, and on this finding the question is one of penalty. The maximum penalty under the Statute is three months' imprisonment, but under my extended power under the Summary Jurisdiction Act, 1879,

in lieu of imprisonment I fine the defendant £5, and £25 costs.

So saying, he granted leave to appeal the decision in a higher court, remarking that he 'would be very glad to see the whole question thoroughly threshed out'.

The second 'bomb' that fell into the astrological camp shortly afterwards was Leo's decision, announced in the next issue of *Modern Astrology*, *not* to appeal. Many astrologers, perhaps most, were flabbergasted and, anticipating that response, Leo and Barley attempted to explain. Firstly, they said, it must be admitted that however unrepresentative, the sentence that had most offended the public prosecutor was indeed predictive. That subjected any appeal to considerable uncertainty. Secondly, wrote Leo, and this was 'the reason why all genuine astrologers must for the time being abide by this Mansion House decision':

> There has been too much loose and irresponsible prediction by a few professional astrologers who have not only been reckless in their language, but also we regret to say immoral in their statements, proof positive of which we received (in private) during the process of our case. And in the face of this sad realisation we are only too well aware that to allow these persons unbridled licence, as might have been the case had the summons been dismissed, would prove utterly fatal to the immediate welfare of Astrology.

(It might well be replied, of course, that if its abuse represented a fatal threat, astrology had already died a thousand deaths.) Thirdly, and more pragmatically, it was hinted that the legal costs, amounting to about fifty pounds a day, were objectionable, if not insurmountable.

The issue was not the taking of money. Reflecting a change in tactics by the public prosecutor, the summons was brought — and allowed to stand, said Leo, as a test case — solely on the charge not of deceiving and imposing but of telling fortunes; and in any case, as he remarked with unusual asperity, the idea that astrologers should not charge for their time and effort was 'sanctimonious nonsense'. Alfred Barley added that it was now clear that 'fortune-telling is making any specific statement about the future'. But since many people of all kinds, business consultants, weather forecasters, etc., make such statements without fear of prosecution, the problem was really the use of astrology to make them. To this problem there was still no simple solution. The public frequently wanted super-natural predictions; the educated mainstream condemned them. To wean both away from such a conception of astrology was far beyond one man's or even one organization's resources. Therefore all that astrologers could do was to offer no such purchase, no chinks in their armour. For that reason, as Barley wrote; 'Astrology, if it is to flourish in this country, must be shorn altogether of its predictive side.'

The truth was, Leo had also decided not to appeal because he saw that it would not address that central problem. And since the re-education of public and élite opinion could not be achieved by force, as it were, he decided that he must start again with what *was* under his control: his own work. As Leo's colleague H. S. Green put it, after the Mansion House prosecution:

> It became evident that his whole system of reading horoscopes would have to be revised, because what he regarded as no more than truthful and legitimate advice to clients the law insisted upon treating as fortune-telling. Therefore he decided to recast the whole system and make it run along the lines of character reading and less as the assertion of an inevitable destiny; referring to events as for the most part a natural outcome of the type of character, which most of them actually are. This entailed a tremendous amount of rewriting of reference-books and sheets.

Of course, Leo had already long inveighed against what he saw as astrology's fatalistic and materialistic tendencies; his crusade was to modernize astrology, in large part, by getting rid of such 'residues'. As Barley admitted; 'This question of foreseeing the future — at its best, was it ever more than a lure, a bait to tempt the unthinking to a study of astrology?' Leo's conviction for fortune-telling really only pushed him further down the same road.

Green was correct when he stated that rewriting hundreds of pages to eliminate any lingering attachment to predictions and events promised a great amount of work. The Leo's had already decided to rent a small cottage at 10 Burn View in the Cornish seaside town of Bude, for a much-needed holiday in August. Typically, however, Leo took all the work with him and spent five hours a day on it. At one point, Bessie objected: 'Why don't you send some of that to Mr Green to do? You are overworking yourself — you will break down.' He replied; 'No, he would take too long. This has to be done quickly, and I must do it myself.'

On the morning of 27 August, Leo complained of feeling unwell. He had a tightness in his chest, he said, and swollen glands and he was running a temperature. The doctor, called a day later, was reassuring; Leo had a bad chill, but would be fine in two or three days. On the morning of the 30th, however, he had convulsions and was violently sick. He apologized to the doctor, whom Bessie had summoned again, and asked him; 'Am I going to die, doctor? I don't mind if I am, I'm not afraid of death.' 'No, certainly not, Mr Leo,' came the archetypal reply, 'you will be quite alright bye and bye.' Ninety minutes later, Leo had another violent fit and passed out. His heart stopped at 10 a.m.; the cause of death was a brain haemorrhage. His 'three years' were up.

Two years later, Bessie, Green and other colleagues and admirers of Leo published a book of biographical reminiscences. Florence Higgs, the secretary of his 'lessons department', recalled:

> There comes to my mind a dream that he told me he had had during the early days of July while the Mansion-House case was pending. In his dream he found himself walking by the sea-shore, carrying something in his hand, and looking at it he became conscious that it was lifeless, and so said to himself, it's no use carrying a *dead* thing, and threw it far into the sea. He watched it splash into the water and disappear, but from the place of its disappearance there came up a water bird, whose head shone with vivid peacock blue colouring; and it swam to the land and walked about, shaking itself free of the water and growing larger and more brilliant as he watched it.

Perhaps Leo had already sensed the trial's probable outcome and the phoenix-like bird represented his hopes for an astrology reborn. Or was the dream a premonition of his own imminent death?

Alan Leo was a sincere, moral and hard-working man. True, he was no giant intellect; as Green wrote, when he first knew Leo: 'Except Madame Blavatsky's *Isis Unveiled* and *The Secret Doctrine*, which he studies seriously, and Raphael's *Guides*, he never interested himself much in any books.' He knew this, of course, and in a familiar move among popular occultists built some protection into his system: 'We attach far more value to one word of the true occultist than a thousand of those who are merely intellectual, and scholars from the physical standpoint alone.' On the other hand, these are also the sentiments, suitably adapted, of many writers, artists and musicians about critics.

Leo also seems to have been almost unable to open his mouth without saying something trite or banal: 'Take it all as just a vibration'; 'It's all experience, and therefore must be for the best'; and so on. But to emphasize these aspects would be to miss the larger point. His tendency to oversimplify was of a piece with his ability to keep his theories simple, for example, 'Character is Destiny'. As the proverbial American preacher advised, Leo 'told 'em what he was going to say, then he said it, and then he told 'em what he'd said'. That knack was central to his genius for, to a remarkable extent, Leo succeeded in his ambition to 'modernize' astrology. He did so by integrating popular astrology with esoteric occultism. The result was an enduring new creation: astrology as a kind of popular, or rather, broadly middle-class occultism.

CONCLUSIONS

LOOKING BACK OVER THIS HISTORY, we can see that 'modernising the ancient system of astrology' was a slow and difficult process that began much earlier. Taking each principal character in turn, it was not something that interested John Varley in the slightest. Indeed, his astrology, in all its unfashionable glory, was radically anti-modern. Varley's other preoccupation was esoteric magic, and this too was still only practised by, and available to, a tiny minority of the relatively well-off and well-educated but disenchanted.

Impelled by his own very different considerations, Raphael took the momentous step of combining magic with the mass-circulation popular astrological almanac. The result was a new kind of almanac, emblematic of an urban and middle-class astrology. It was soon seized upon and expanded, with considerable success, by Zadkiel. Ironically, given how much their moral and intellectual leaders detested him, what made Zadkiel's success possible was the very strength of the Victorian middle classes. Their complexity, diversity and independence resulted in the creation of their own new occult underworld. In an age, furthermore, that was 'destitute of faith, but terrified at scepticism', as Carlyle put it, many people were ready for an exotic new prophet.

But this process was still incomplete. Although they could now be found in the same pages, magic (crystal-ball gazing, angelic orders, and so forth) on the one hand and astrology on the other remained relatively unintegrated. So too did Zadkiel's scientific and astronomical speculations. His successor, A. J. Pearce, and Richard

Garnett both struggled to rejoin them by bringing astrology back into the fold of science, but in vain: even after three centuries, the pariah still was not welcome. Nor, understandably, did scientists appreciate Alan Leo's efforts to accomplish the reverse integration, by redescribing their vocation as a shallow and materialistic branch of true esoteric science. Leo also met with internal resistance from astrologers like Pearce and Garnett, who could not stomach esotericism, or at least, like Sepharial, his and Bessie's version of it.

Leo's masterstroke, however — and even allowing for its limitations and dissenters, where he did succeed — was to wed the new middle-class astrology to esoteric magic in the form of Theosophy. Amid dissolving older religious certainties and widespread worries about the new scientific ones, combined with an ever-increasing emphasis on the subjective self as traditional social connections loosened and dissolved, Leo's move was perfectly timed. It offered people, in the words of the proverbial marriage charm, something old, something new, something borrowed, and, politically speaking, something blue.

What has happened since? In a nutshell, Theosophy, in the sense of the precise teachings of the Theosophical Society, has rather dropped out of the picture; while astrology, that extraordinarily tough 'crazy old lady', obviously has not. In addition to the popular sun-sign columns in tabloid newspapers everywhere, socially speaking astrology is still chiefly a broadly middling, 'semi-erudite' concern. But its focus is overwhelmingly psychological rather than explicitly spiritual. For a few, astrology is a way of life: something that can be either deeply fulfilling or neurotically needed, as the case may be. For most people who are aware of its existence, however, it is but one option for personal self-development in a dazzling array dominated by psychoanalysis, alternative therapies and the latest New Age movement, which began in the early 1980s. To some extent, astrology has itself become the psychology ('Sun in Capricorn makes you ambitious') as well as the meta-history ('the Age of Aquarius') of the New Age movement as a whole. This process began with the counter-culture of the 1960s and, as that became increasingly tamed and accepted, re-packaged and marketed, so too did astrology.

Theosophical astrology did not simply disappear, however, nor did the psychological variety appear out of nowhere. Its spiritual and esoteric content was in fact deliberately remade in the image of the latter. Leo's motto, 'Character is Destiny', had already moved the spotlight from using the stars to tell people's fortunes to 'reading' their character. From there it was but a short step from an occult 'inner world' to a psyche. Thus an afflicted Saturn no longer signifies karmic difficulties so much as an internalized repressive father-figure, Mars represents libido, etc.

This take-over left the Theosophical framework almost intact, except that it was now made safe, so to speak, for democracy. That is, it satisfied people's need for 'deep meaning' while appearing safely secular and even, to the indignation of scientific apologists and publicists, perhaps scientific. The guiding light in this development was the 'depth psychology' of Carl Jung. It began in 1936 with the appearance of a book called *The Astrology of Personality* by Dane Rudhyar, a naturalized American astrologer. Rudhyar acted as a direct link between Theosophy, in particular that of Alice Bailey, and Jung. In 'humanistic' and later 'transpersonal' astrology, the nativity came to represent a map of the psyche, revealing a person's deepest archetypal constellations of anima and animus, shadow, self, and so on. With a leg-up from the *Zeitgeist* of the 1960s and '70s, Rudhyar's vision of astrology spread far and wide from its native California. Indeed, it was but one part of what has been called world-wide Californication.

This compromise between astrology and psychology reminds one of another accommodation seven centuries earlier, with the vastly influential synthesis of Christianity and Greek natural philosophy wrought by Thomas Aquinas. Just as before, the new arrangement has given astrology yet another lease of life, as well as undeniably enriching it in many ways. Also as before, however, something has been lost: a certain charm, precision and power of symbolism that was still very much evident in the craft of Varley. His successors too occasionally demonstrated such an ability, but by the time of Alan Leo it had already become rare. As the poet Michael Longley observed of art: 'When you capture something with precision, you also release its mysterious aura.

You don't get the mystery without the precision.' Although I have no doubt they survive here and there in practice, in the massed ranks of contemporary astrological textbooks, with their cookbook formulae and stale prose, there is precious little precision or mystery.

The deal has also extracted another price, namely a significant loss of independence, relatively speaking, as a tradition and a practice. As we have seen, of course, astrology's survival has traditionally depended a great deal on its ability to adapt to more powerful discourses. But, to that extent, astrology's ability to offer a genuine alternative is compromised. Perhaps this is one reason why, in 1989, the legal apparatus restricting astrology to 'pretending or professing' could safely be dropped; as merely a part of the common psychological domain, it could now be ignored, or at least tolerated.

In the process, astrology has continued to acquire a political passivity and conservatism that could not be further removed from its seventeenth-century reputation for wild-eyed radicalism. That reputation continues to haunt astrology as a ghost in the upper rooms of the social mansion; but it is nameless. As the earlier period demonstrates, however, such quietism is not inherent in astrology. Such things never are, depending rather on historical context.

In the nineteenth century, astrology had already been marginalized, and was well on its way to being thoroughly depoliticized. Partly for that reason, this tale has been in some ways a quaint one of curious people, although no more curious, in fact, than most of their contemporaries. It was not particularly quaint for the principal characters, however. Their struggles and sufferings were real enough at the time and frequently included a brush with higher powers: not the purely spiritual kind, but the sort we encounter more often in our daily lives.

Organized religion, institutionalized science and the state are among the major players in modern social life. When they join hands in the name of 'truth', or even just 'common sense', the usual result is a largely tacit but strong sense not just of what matters, but also of what is possible, of what is worth discussing and pursuing and what is not. Despite the ever-increasing contribution of modern science to this consensus, the latter has nothing to do with evidence in the strict scientific sense — either now or, as we have seen, in the nineteenth century. The facts never 'speak for themselves', but whether they are members of the intellectual mainstream or on its margins, those who are aware of the rhetorical function of facts remain in a minority.

Throughout history, some people have had the temerity to insist on differing from predominant views. When the differences turned on points that both the dissenters and the authorities felt to be crucial, the upshot was often very dangerous for the former. Many among the more determined, or just unlucky, have paid dearly: Bruno dying at the stake in 1600 was not the first, nor Wilhelm Reich in prison in 1957 the last, and there have been many 'poor Pagans under the hedge' in between. In this context, our astrologers were probably fortunate to have escaped as lightly as they did.

On the whole, of course, they showed a healthy instinct for self-preservation. The ones who had least, such as Zadkiel, suffered the most. But that instinct was allied, I would argue, to a professional dynamic or characteristic, and one which can fittingly be described in their own terms. There is a place in the symbolism of the horoscope for everything, and astrologers themselves are traditionally 'ruled' by Mercury. Mercury or Hermes is the god who acts as cosmic go-between, linking the other gods and goddesses with human beings. As such, he signifies diviners of all kinds, dealing in messages and meanings, but he is also the god of thieves, tricksters and apparent fools. His ability to convey divine messages thus coexists with a well-deserved reputation for chameleon-like adaptability and occasional unreliability. In a word, he is mercurial.

This is not a figure to trade thunderbolts or take centre-stage, but rather one to lead a merry chase. He can order the universe for you in a flash; but not to order. And like their god — or, to take a more natural metaphor, like an animal which is also linked with Mercury: the fox — astrologers are at their best when enlivening, quickening and disappearing. Few are foolish enough to try to stand their ground with the dogs.

Left unhunted, as it were, being a good astrologer is probably comparable to being a good musician, or mechanic, or monk. Anyone can study the subject, and even use it; but without some talent, as well as persistence, you will not get very far. Like all other human beings, however, astrologers are affected by many other considerations arising from living in a particular society at a particular time. Thus, these Victorian and Edwardian astrologers' understanding of what they were doing had limits we need no longer feel bound by.

One such limit, shared by such otherwise very divergent practitioners, was an abhorrence of 'horary' astrology. That is the practice, very popular in the seventeenth century and still known now, of answering a query on the basis of a map of the heavens for the moment it was asked or received. For Leo, 'Horary astrology, as practised today, is the vilest rubbish imaginable, and not worthy of the name. Indeed, it is not astrology at all, but simply divination, for which purpose geomancy or card laying would answer just as well . . . IT IS THE CURSE OF THE SCIENCE AND THE RUIN OF THE ASTROLOGER.' Strong words, from a normally mild man and a leading representative of Theosophy! Or was Leo especially sensitive on just that account? Pearce, who had always upheld the ideals of science, merely blamed astrology's low ebb in recent centuries on 'the absurd and unwarrantable use made of the horary branch of it, in the Middle Ages'.

Despite the difference in tone, however, the extent of agreement is striking. What was going on here? The distinctive thing about horary astrology has always been its lack of an easily conceivable 'rational' or material basis. Nativities and even inceptional maps, done for the beginning of a project, can always invoke the idea of births, seeds, blueprints and similar analogies. This kind of rhetorical protection is simply not available for horaries and, as a result, they stand out, inviting attacks as superstitious, ignorant, irrational, and so on. In short, as astrology stands to science, so horary stands to astrology.

Astrology was therefore 'cursed' in its search for acceptance and respectability by a family member that was plainly and simply divinatory and, as such, acceptable to almost no one. Yet the attempt to disown horary now seems something of a craven sop to those who will, in any event, never be satisfied. Indeed, horary astrology has recently seen a resurgence in England which upholds it as the very heart of astrological practice. This move, which turns an embarrassing black sheep into the head of the family, seems a more satisfying and even honest account. Astrology does indeed take its place alongside card-laying, geomancy and other kinds of divination — the difference being, and it is an important one, that in the West, at least, astrology embodies a uniquely old, stable and sophisticated tradition of divination, whose system is unmatched for both subtlety and rigour. As the eighteenth-century scholar William Stukeley put it, 'There is something in it so agreeable to nature, to the chequerwork of life, that . . . it strikes a considering mind with great pleasure.' (Indeed, an unconsidering mind can find much in it as well.)

Understanding how divination works, when it does, may present an enormous, even unanswerable challenge. So too does the problem of maintaining standards, based on an appropriate concept of evidence that has not been arbitrarily transposed from another tradition, usually that of science. Understanding the presence of divination, however, does not. It is the way human beings have always sought advice when there is no simple or obvious solution. The paradigmatic divinatory question is, would such-and-such course of action have the blessing of the gods? Such a question is invariably highly practical and concrete in its content. Paradoxically, it acknowledges the sense that ultimately, after all our efforts to comprehend and manipulate, events are not finally under our control; that there is a determining aspect of life, traditionally character-ized as divine or supernatural, which is literally beyond us. Viewed this way, it is as fundamental and universal a part of the human condition as is possible in this changeable sublunary world. And when one finds oneself in a situation where that condition is paramount, divination is then potentially as practical and 'rational' a response as any. That is not to say, of course, that it is always, or even often, an appropriate course of action. None the less, it merits rather more attention, as well as respect, than it usually receives.

Divining for purposes of prediction, though common enough, is secondary in this sense: the question, What is going to happen? is actually an implicit attempt to learn what to do if it *does* happen, and thus what attitude to assume now. And even in its most mundane and predictive form, as was often the case with Varley and occasionally with his successors, divination can serve to remind us that, in the words of the novelist Josef Skvorecky, 'At the bottom of human life, there is a mystery, and all simple answers to it, whether they are political or whatever, are simply silly. The point of art,' he adds, 'is to remind us of that.' Skvorecky's words may serve also to remind us that divination has much in common with artistic and mythopoeic — literally, myth-making — acts of imagination.

Of course, divining is not simply an individual or arbitrary act, but a highly social one; it requires training in interpretation, without which its results are literally meaningless. That in turn is impossible without a living tradition of past interpretations and a contemporary community of fellow practitioners mutually to criticize and correct. However, even allowing for its much greater resources, institutionalization and effects, the same is just as true for a more famous attempt to fly in the face of the ineffable and obtain knowledge that will give us control over our lives. I am thinking, of course, of modern science. This gives rise to a curious thought: suppose that at the very heart of the modern Western scientific project — with its rationalism, materialism and instrumentalism that is still being exported all over the world as the solution to all the problems in more 'primitive' and benighted parts — there lies an act of divination?

In which case; alongside astrology and other traditional forms of knowledge, as the science that dare not speak its name, we have the reverse: a science committed to denying and disguising its common origins in an act that precisely acknowledges human fallibility, limitations and mystery. Perhaps the craving of science to establish and monopolize the truth, and therefore much of its reckless destructiveness, is even a consequence, to some extent, of this attitude. There is something deeply Faustian about it all: extraordinary powers and pleasures, in return for the soul; indeed, for the very idea of soul. A very small price, the modern Mesphisto whispers. But this is not something I want to assert so much as a question I want to pose, in order to see how things look in its light.

Modern astrology is also partly an understandable reaction against modernity and its cult of progress. A sense of isolation and alienation; the growing debris of social and ecological destruction; boredom, aimlessness and helplessness — such concerns are none the less valid for not being new. I could not convey the appeal of astrology against this backdrop better than the Reverend James 'Shepherd' Smith, writing in 1848:

> An astrologer is an artist, an astronomer is not . . . astrology puts a spirit into nature and a poetical meaning into all its movements, and the philosophy that extinguishes this spirit, and sneers at this poetical meaning, extinguishes and sneers at the human soul itself, and reduces man, as it reduces nature, to a material mass, governed by stupid chemical agents, acting from no intelligent motive and tending to no definite or positive result. Hence the people are leaving faith; and the clergy themselves are going along with them, carried away by the tide though anxious to stem it, but not knowing how far they themselves are engaged unwittingly in the crusade against believers.

Viewed in this way, astrology is but a wave on a swell of concern that continues from the nineteenth century into our own. It is growing, but the swell is still contradicted by a sea of short-term politics, worship of money, and unrestrained scientific technology, which still seems to be rushing in the direction of mutual and global self-destruction. That is encouraging for the future of astrology, I suppose, but less so for that of life on earth.

Compared to the prime movers of this situation, both past and present, astrologers are of course the merest scapegoats whose human interest I hope I have shown. In the end, however, astrologers' only protection, and it is a flimsy and fragile one, is our common right to live, think and act as we wish, unqualified except by an equal duty to uphold the right of others to do likewise. Ironically, that right was most resoundingly proclaimed by Zadkiel's contemporary, and probably the most famously secular and rationalist man of his time, John Stuart Mill. But his vision of the freedom of the individual from the tyranny of the majority opinion far transcended its nineteenth-century origins. In a way that chimes resoundingly with both ancient polytheism and post-modern relativism, he was acutely aware, in the words of a modern exponent, 'of the many-sidedness of the truth and of the irreducible complexity of life'. Against the self-aggrandizement of the powerful and simple, Mill perceived the value of the fragile, complex and useless — whether human or natural. In the late twentieth century, our ability to translate his vision into a life-affirming ethic for the whole biosphere has become crucial. At stake is the difference between mere survival, at best, and a life worth living — for all of us.

The weakness of liberal pluralism is that it rarely provides us with what actually makes life worth living. That, once survival can be assumed, tends to consist of satisfactions rooted in the kind of cultural values that are ultimately spiritual, if not necessarily religious. Granted their right to a place under the Sun, then, there may be some things that astrologers are unusually well placed to teach us: a sense of wonder; an awareness of belonging to an intelligent universe, made up of qualities as well as quantity; an appreciation of cycles, continuities and responsibilities. There are many other teachers, of course, and these are not the only lessons. But they are becoming urgent.

REFERENCES

Introduction

Note: *The Dictionary of National Biography* (Oxford: Oxford University Press, 1921–7, 22 vols), is abbreviated to *DNB*.

I am grateful to John Heath-Stubbs for pointing out Sir Walter Scott's astrology to me. The quotations from *Guy Mannering* are from pp. 8 and 52–3. (Astrology is also present in another, near-contemporary novel, J. H. Shorthouse's *John Inglesant*. Shorthouse's use of it, however, reveals that, unlike Scott, he had a very poor grasp of the subject.)

I should add that concentrating on London means that some other nineteenth-century astrologers of merit have unfortunately been neglected: especially Luke Dennis Broughton (1829–99), who was born in Leeds but spent most of his professional life in Philadelphia and New York City; William Joseph Simmonite (*fl.* 1837–61) of Sheffield; and George Wilde (1860–*c*.1914), initially of Brighouse, Yorkshire. All three men published works on astrology.

My *Prophecy and Power: Astrology in Early Modern England* (1989), which covers the period antecedent to the present book, is published in Britain by Polity Press and in North America by Princeton University Press. It also contains a more thorough discussion of the historiographical and epistemological issues involved in the history of 'pseudo-science'. See also my 'Astrology in Early Modern England: The Making of a Vulgar Knowledge' in *Science, Culture and Popular Belief*, ed. S. Pumphrey, P. Rossi and M. Slawinski (Manchester: Manchester University Press, 1991). Readers interested in this earlier period should also look out for Ann Geneva's *Astrology and the Seventeenth-Century Mind: William Lilly and the Language of the Stars* (Berkeley: University of California Press, 1993).

The quotation by Washington Irving comes from W. D. Rubinstein, *Elites and the Wealthy in Modern British History: Essays in Social and Economic History* (Brighton: Harvester Press, 1987), p. 312. The description of 'Professor Smith' is from the Rev. Charles Maurice Smith, *Mystic London: or, Phases of*

Occult Life in the Metropolis (London: Tinsley Bros, 1875). The words of the socially upwardly mobile almanac come from *Old Moore's Monthly Messenger* I:1 (October 1907), p. 13.

For some sales figures for almanacs in the nineteenth century, see Abel Heywood, *Three Papers on English Printed Almanacs* (London: privately printed, 1904). The work, otherwise excellent, of Asa Briggs will suffice as an example of how astrology in nineteenth-century England has been missed or passed over. The sole exception seems to be a single chapter — albeit elegant and scrupulous — in the late Ellic Howe's *Astrology and the Third Reich* (Wellingborough: Aquarian Press, 1984) which was first published as *Urania's Children: The Strange World of the Astrologers* (1967).

For the 1989 repeal of the part of the Vagrancy Act used against astrologers, see 'The Law Commission and the Scottish Law Commission, Statute Law Revision: Thirteenth Report', pp. 10, 69.

For a wonderful portrayal of surviving 'popular' belief in the stars in the nineteenth century — albeit on the part of an extraordinary individual, namely the shepherd Robert Dellanow (also known as 'Snarley Bob') — see L. P. Jacks, *Mad Shepherds* (Oxford: Oxford University Press, 1979; first published 1910). This book reveals the strange commonality of belief in the stars between the popular and the 'high' traditions of Neoplatonism and Gnosticism, and the gulf between both of those kinds of astrology and the more individualistic middle-class astrology that is principally my subject here.

Books discussing other 'occult' beliefs in this period include Janet Oppenheim, *Spiritualism and Psychical Research in England, 1850–1914* (Cambridge: Cambridge University Press, 1985); Logie Barrow, *Independent Spirits: Spiritualism and English Plebeians, 1850–1910* (London: Routledge & Kegan Paul, 1986); Roger Cooter, *The Cultural Meaning of Popular Science* (Cambridge: Cambridge University Press, 1984); and Alex Owen, *The Darkened Room: Women, Power and Spiritualism in Late Victorian England* (London: Virago, 1989).

The quotation from Barrington Moore, Jr is from his *Social Origins of Dictatorship and Democracy* (London: Allen Lane, 1967), p. 523. 'I believe in their belief' was suggested to me by a scene in a film, 'A Month in the Country', based on J. L. Carr's novel of the same name, in which someone restoring a medieval painting of the Last Judgement is asked whether he 'believes' in it. He replies: 'When I am working on it, I believe in his [that is, the artist's] belief.'

Incidentally, respecting that belief, I have tried to supply the times of birth for each of the astrologers, as they themselves would have appreciated, and modern ones still will.

John Varley

I am grateful to Roger Parisious for first introducing me to John Varley as an astrologer. In this connection, I should mention that he intends to publish an extended commentary on W. B. Yeats and astrology, which may include some reference to Varley's 'lost' manuscript.

The principal sources of information which I have used for Varley — his life, astrology and prophecies — are as follows: his own *Zodiacal Physiognomy* (London: privately printed, 1828); John Lewis Roget, *A History of the 'Old Water-Colour' Society, now the Royal Society of Painters in Water Colours* (London: Longmans, Green and Co., 1891), 2 vols; Alfred T. Story, *James Holmes and John Varley* (London: Richard Bentley and Son, 1894) and *The Life of John Linnell* (London: Richard Bentley and Son, 1892), 2 vols; Adrian Bury, *John Varley of the 'Old Society'* (Leigh-on-Sea: F. Lewis, 1946); 'Some Astrological Predictions of the Late John Varley, by his grandson John Varley, with Introduction by A. P. Sinnett', *The Occult Review* XXIV:1 (July 1916) 38–43; 'John Varley', *DNB* vol. XX, pp. 150–3; Richard and Samuel Redgrave, *A Century of Painters of the English School* (London: Smith, Elder and Co., 1866), 2 vols; and handwritten transcriptions, in the possession of The Old Water-Colour Society's Club at the Bankside Gallery, London, of several short manuscripts: 'Reminiscences of John Varley, by J. P. Neale', 'By Cornelius Varley', 'Mr Ward's Account of Varley', 'At Mrs Smith's' and a few other oddments. I also consulted some of Varley's few surviving letters in the Victoria and Albert Museum Library. A recent work on Varley, which touches on his astrology, is C. M. Kauffmann, *John Varley, 1778–1842* (London: Batsford, 1984).

Other sources I have consulted are: Grantley F. Berkeley, *My Life and Recollections* (London: Hurst and Bleckett, 1865–6), 4 vols; John Sartain, *The Reminiscences of a Very Old Man, 1808–1897* (New York: D. Appleworth, 1899); Frederic G. Stephens, *Memorials of William Mulready, R.A.* (London: Sampson Lowe, Marston, Searle and Rivington, 1890) and *Masterpieces of Mulready* (London: Bell and Daldy, 1867); *Exhibition of Drawings in Water Colours by Artists Anterior to 1800* (London: Burlington Fine Arts Club, 1871); *Annals of the Fine Arts, for 1817* vol. II (London: Sherwood, Neely and Jones, 1818); Sydney D. Kitson, *The Life of John Sell Cotman* (London: Faber, 1837); Allan Cunningham, *The Lives of the Most Eminent British Painters* (London: George Bell, 1879–80), 3 vols; *The Sheepshanks Gallery* (London: Bell and Daldy, 1870); and A. H. Palmer, *The Life and Letters of Samuel Palmer, Painter and Etcher* (London: Sealey, 1838). *The Phrenological Journal* XVI (Edinburgh: 1843), p. 195 includes a report of a meeting on 20 February that year, at which Varley's phrenological character was discussed. Burton's account comes from Alfred T. Story, op. cit., pp. 253–4; and from Isabel Burton, *The Life of Captain Sir Richard Burton*, vol. I (London: Chapman & Hall, 1893), 2 vols, I, p. 16. The Constable episode comes from *The Letters of John Constable, R.A. to C. R. Leslie, R.A. 1826–1837*, ed. Peter Leslie

(London: Constable, 1931). Varley's lisp is mentioned in *Georgiana's Journal, Melbourne 1841–1865*, ed. Hugh McCrae (London: Angus & Robertson, 1967, 2nd edn), p. xix.

Some of Varley's exact addresses mentioned above were at 15 (and later 5) Broad Street; 44 Conduit Street; and 10½ Great Titchfield Street.

Ruskin's account comes from E. T. Cook and Alexander Wedderburn, *The Works of John Ruskin* (London: George Allen & Unwin, 1903–12), 39 vols, XXXV, p. 298, n.1. Ruskin noted his own birth-time as 'half past seven a.m. (under Aquarius)' on 8 February 1819, in Bloomsbury – from E. T. Cook, *The Life of John Ruskin*, (London: George Allen & Unwin, 1911), 2 vols., I, p. 6. Ruskin's views on the Sun come from Dinah Birch, '"The Sun is God": Ruskin's Solar Mythology', pp. 109–23 in ed. J. B. Bullen, *The Sun is God: Painting, Literature and Mythology in the Nineteenth Century* (Oxford: Clarendon Press, 1989). The quotation by Max Müller comes from Gillian Beer's '"The Death of the Sun": Victorian Solar Physics and Solar Myth', pp. 159–80 in the same volume.

The source for Varley's birth-data is Raphael (i.e. Robert Cross Smith) in *The Astrologer of the Nineteenth Century* (London: Knight and Lacey, 1825), pp. 432–4. The time given by Raphael results in an ascendant of 18° 19′ Sagittarius; however, Blake's drawing of Varley (National Portrait Gallery No. 1194) is inscribed 'John Varley Born August 17, 1778, 18.56 Sagittarius ascending'. According to Kauffmann, another inscription formerly on the mount of Varley's 'Demolition of Hackney Church' gave 18° 54′. (It is rare to be in possession of one's precise time of birth, usually but not necessarily the first breath, and these minor discrepancies are a typical preoccupation of practising astrologers.) Varley and Smith were clearly acquainted. In the latter's *Urania; or the Astrologer's Chronicle, and Mystical Magazine* I (1825) he also supplies the birth-data for Blake — 7.45 a.m., 28 November 1757, London — remarking: 'We have been in company with this gentleman several times.'

The comment about the readership of Varley's book was by Godfrey Barker in 'Forgotten Blake drawings found', the *Daily Telegraph*, 10 February 1989. Adrian Bury says that a prospectus for the sequel is in the Victoria and Albert Museum Library, in a volume entitled 'Fine Arts Pamphlets, 1801–1874'. Unfortunately, it cannot now be traced there, under that or any other name. Note also that there is a problem with the date of William Mulready's final letter that Bury cites; namely that it just postdates its writer's death! Unless the commonly accepted date of death is wrong, I assume that Bury has made a simple error in his transcription.

For Varley and William Blake, the additional sources were: Martin Butlin, *The Blake-Varley Sketchbook of 1819* (London: Heinemann, 1969), 2 vols; *The Larger Blake-Varley Sketchbook, which will be sold at Christie's Great Rooms on Tuesday 21 March 1989 at 12.45 p.m. approximately* (London: Christie, Manson and Woods Ltd, 1989); Alexander Gilchrist, *Life of William Blake* (London: J. M. Dent, 1863); G. E. Bentley, Jr, *Blake Records* (Oxford: Clarendon Press, 1969) and *Blake Books: Annotated Catalogues of William Blake's Writings* (Oxford: Clarendon Press, 1977). There is an interesting discussion in Fred Gettings, *The Hidden Art: A Study of Occult Symbolism in Art* (London: Studio Vista, 1978), pp. 109–26.

Additional sources for the Blessingtons and their circle were as follows: in general, Michael Sadleir, *Blessington-D'Orsay. A Masquerade* (London: Constable, 1933), from which the description of Varley and Disraeli is quoted (p. 261); and Ellen Moers, *The Dandy* (London: Secker & Warburg, 1960). On Lady Blessington (1789–1849), *DNB* II pp. 675–7. (A letter from Varley to Robert Balmanno, dated 31 March 1822, refers to a future dinner engagement with the Earl of Blessington.)

There is a surviving nativity for Bulwer-Lytton, possibly drawn up by Zadkiel, which is set for 6 a.m. on Wednesday, 25 May 1803, near London. (His son comments: 'The year and the day of the month are correctly stated in it. The day of the week and the hour of the day may possibly be correct also. But my father was undoubtedly born in London' — at 31 Portman Square *in* the West End — 'not near it.') However, Richard Garnett, who was scrupulous about such things, points out that Bulwer-Lytton himself says that he was born at 8 a.m., the time which should therefore be preferred; see his letter of 10 December 1904, reprinted in *Modern Astrology* XVII/III:7 (July 1906), pp. 304–5.

For Bulwer-Lytton (1803–73), including his nativity, I have used *DNB* XII, pp. 380–7; *The Life, Letters and Literary Remains of Edward Bulwer, Lord Lytton, by his son* (London: Kegan Paul, 1883), 2 vols; *The Life of Edward Bulwer, First Lord Lytton, by his grandson the Earl of Lytton* (London: Macmillan, 1913), 2 vols; Robert Lee Wolff, *Strange Stories and Other Explorations in Victorian Fiction* (Boston: Garnbit, 1971); C. Nelson Stewart, *Bulwer Lytton as Occultist* (London: Theosophical Publishing House, 1927); and the novels I have mentioned. Bulwer-Lytton's experience with the gypsies comes from the grandson's *Life*, I, 101–2; his geomantic figure concerning Disraeli, from his son's *Life*, II, p. 238, and Stewart, pp. 26–7. There was an earlier reference to Bulwer's nativity by Zadkiel in his *Handbook of Astrology* I (London: G. Berger, 1861), I, p. 11. For another example of Bulwer-Lytton's strange migration from fiction into (spiritual) 'fact', see Rudolph Steiner's reference to the 'Guardian of the Threshold' in *Zanoni*, in his *Knowledge of the Higher Worlds* (London: Rudolph Steiner Press, 1969), p. 196.

On the influence of Bulwer-Lytton on Blavatsky, see S. B. Liljegren, 'Bulwer-Lytton's Novels and *Isis Unveiled*', in *Essays and Studies on English Language and Literature* XVIII (1957), 7–60; and V. S. Solovyoff, *A Modern Priestess of Isis*, trans. Walter Leaf (London: Longmans Green and Co., 1895). The quotation from Blavatsky on Bulwer-Lytton is in her *Isis Unveiled: A Master-Key to the Mysteries of Ancient and Modern Science and Theology*, (New York: J. W. Bouton, 1877, 2nd edn), 2 vols., I, pp. 285–6.

The passage concerning scientists is by Professor Robert Edwards in *Experiments on Embryos*, ed. Anthony Dyson and John Harris (London: Routledge & Kegan Paul, 1990), as quoted in the *Times Literary Supplement*, 27 April–3 May 1990.

I have gratefully borrowed the expression 'authorized prophets', and not for the first time, from Simon Schaffer, 'Authorized Prophets: Comets and Astronomers After 1759', *Studies in Eighteenth Century Culture* XVII (1987), pp. 45–74; he was in turn quoting the late eighteenth-century astronomer J. H. Lambert.

For Thomas Dick (1774–1857), in addition to the book mentioned, see *DNB* V, pp. 923. For Augustus Frederick (1773–1843), see *DNB* I 729–30; John Hamill, *The Craft. A History of English Freemasonry* (Wellingborough: Crucible, 1986); and Adrian Bury, op. cit.

Zadkiel's purchase of Lady Blessington's crystal ball was described by a contemporary, Frederick Hockley, in a paper delivered on 14 April 1873, and quoted in John Hamill, *The Rosicrucian Seer: Magical Writing of Frederick Hockley* (Wellingborough: Aquarian Press, 1986), pp. 132–3. Zadkiel also described the crystal as originally hers, e.g. in his *Zadkiel's Almanac for 1851*.

Raphael

The basic sources I have used for Raphael's life and work are, of course, his own books, as mentioned above, and almanac, *The Prophetic Messenger*. (In 1840, the publication's name was changed to *Raphael's Prophetic Messenger*, and still later *Almanac*.) There are also two obituaries by contemporaries: Dixon, writing in *The True Prophetic Messenger for 1833*, pp. 84–93, and Zadkiel, i.e. Richard James Morrison, writing in Raphael's *The Royal Book of Fate* (London: Sherwood, 1856), pp. xiv–xv. The best secondary source is Ellic Howe's *Raphael, or, The Royal Merlin* (London: Arborfield, 1964) and pp. 28–33 of his excellent *Astrology and the Third Reich* (Wellingborough: Aquarian, 1984), originally published as *Urania's Children: The Strange World of the Astrologers* (London: William Kimber, 1967). Another secondary source for bibliographical information on Raphael and his successors is F. Leigh Gardner, *A Catalogue Raisonné of Works on the Occult Sciences,* (London: privately printed, 1903–12), 3 vols, vol II: *Astrological Books*, 1911.

The opening quotation is from *Raphael's Witch!!!* (London: W. C. Wright, 1831), p. 7. The episode with George IV comes from Raphael, *The Familiar Astrologer* (London: John Bennett, 1831), pp. 513–18; it was repeated in *The Prophetic Messenger for 1832*, pp. 59–62, and *Raphael's Witch!!!* pp. 513–18 as well as *Herschel's Coming Events* I:3 (December 1896, pp. 56–9).

Regarding the fine points of biography: first, for the birth of Smith I have given the time he himself supplied, in his *The Astrologer of the Nineteenth Century*, pp. 435–6. In his obituary in *The Royal Book of Fate*, Zadkiel uses the accompanying horoscope to correct that time to 9.05.20 a.m. In addition, Dixon gives 9.11 a.m., and Palmer, in *The Prophetic Messenger for 1833*, 9.25 a.m. Second, the recorded birth-data (mostly from various editions of *The Prophetic Messenger*) for succeeding Raphaels are as follows: John Palmer (R.II) — 8.29 p.m., 28 May 1807, London?; Medhurst (R. III) — unknown; Wakeley (R. IV, also known as 'Edwin Raphael') — 7.26 a.m., 10 May 1814, latitude 50°N 48' (died 1853); R. V. Sparkes (R. V) — 17 July 1820 (died April 1875); and Robert T. Cross (R. VI) — 2.35 a.m., 15 May 1850, East Anglia (died 1923). Biographical information on Cross comes largely from *The Astrologer's Magazine* XLIV (March 1894), p. 169, and the *British Journal of Astrology* XVI (August 1923), p. 161.

Estimates of sales of *The Prophetic Messenger/Almanac* come from *Raphael's Witch!!!*, p. v; L. D. Broughton, *Elements of Astrology* (London: the author, 1898, p.x); F. Leigh Gardner, pp. 129–30; Alan Leo, *A Critical Dictionary of Astrology* (London: ?, 1905), p. 3; *The Astrologer's Magazine* V (1894–5), p. 53.

On publishing in the nineteenth century, see Richard D. Altick, *Writers, Readers and Occasions: Selected Essays on Victorian Literature and Life* (Columbus OH: Ohio State University Press, 1989). For a description of the political situation, see Adrian Desmond, *The Politics of Evolution: Morphology, Medicine and Reform in Radical London* (Chicago/London: University of Chicago Press, 1989).

The quotation by Bulwer-Lytton is from the Introduction to *Zanoni* (London: George Routledge & Sons, 1853). For information on George Graham, see L. T. C. Holt, *The Aeronauts* (London: Longmans, 1966), pp. 112–14. On Francis Barrett, see E. M. Butler, *Ritual Magic* (Cambridge: Cambridge University Press, 1949), pp. 254–7; John Hamill, *The Rosicrucian Seer: Magical Writings of Frederick Hockley* (Wellingborough: Aquarian Press, 1986), pp. 20–1; and especially R. Heisler, 'Behind "The Magus": Francis Barrett, Magical Balloonist', *The Pentacle* I:4 (1985), pp. 53–7. On John Denley, see Hamill, pp. 11, 21; and F. Leigh Gardner, p. 130.

The quotation by Theodor Adorno comes from his article 'The Stars Down to Earth: The L. A. Times Astrology Column', *Telos* 19 (1974), 13–90, p. 87.

Zadkiel

The basic sources for Zadkiel are his own books and almanacs, as mentioned in the text above; the *DNB* XIII, 1006–8; and Chris Cooke, *Curiosities of Occult Literature* (London: Arthur Hall, Smart and Allen, 1863). The copy of the latter in the British Library is invaluable, as it contains extensive handwritten *addenda* by the author. The only secondary source I know of is Ellic Howe, *Astrology and the Third Reich*, op. cit., which is presumably based on the same sources as those I have used.

In addition to *Zadkiel's Almanac*, he commenced various other short-lived astrological publications: *The Horoscope* (1834, 1841, 1843), *Zadkiel's Magazine* (1849) and *The Voice of the Stars* (1862).

The results of Zadkiel's investigations with the crystal ball are reported in detail in *Zadkiel's Almanac for 1851, 1852* and *1862*.

Newspapers and journals used include the *Daily Telegraph* (31 January, 1862; 1 February, 1862), *The Times* (28 April, 1862; 30 June, 1863; 1 July, 1863), the *Morning Advertiser* (30 June, 1863), the *Saturday Review* (4 July, 1863), the *Sun* (14 February, 1855) the *London Review* (25 October, 1862), the *London Magazine* (1828, vol. II, p. 591), the *Athenaeum* (2 January, 1828; 2 November, 1850; 6 December, 1851; 11 July, 1863) and the *Penny Magazine* (23 September, 1843). For the trial, I have used the two mentioned in the text in that connection; I merged the accounts for that purpose, but changed nothing of any substance.

Zadkiel's birth-data is taken from his *Zadkiel's Almanac for 1846*, p. 48; a handwritten note in the British Library copy notes that Zadkiel had rectified his nativity (here with early Virgo rising) in order to arrive at an ascendant of 28° 04' Leo. However, Cooke, in *Curiosities*, p. 10, gives 9.45 a.m., stating that the resulting nativity 'is correct according to Mr Morrison's statement'. A. J. Pearce also gives 9.45 a.m. in *The Future* II:23 (December 1893), p. 179.

Bulwer-Lytton's letter to Hargraves Jennings appears in *The Life of Edward Bulwer ... by his grandson ...*, (London: Macmillan, 1913), 2 vols, II, p. 42.

The story of Brougham's 'death' comes from P.W. Wilson, ed., *The Greville Diary*, (London: William Heinemann, 1927), 2 vols, I, pp. 531–2. (Thanks to Simon Schaffer for bringing this to my attention.)

Information on W. S. Cross comes from A. G. Trent in *The Horoscope* I:3 (1903), pp. 145–9. On Frederick Hockley, see John Hamill, *The Rosicrucian Seer: Magical Writings of Frederick Hockley* (Wellingborough: Aquarian Press, 1986). Hockley's 'Five Treatises on Magic' is in the Wellcome Institute Library, MS. 3203. On Brown, see Logie Barrow, *Independent Spirits: Spiritualism and English Plebeians, 1850–1910* (London: Routledge & Kegan Paul, 1986), pp. 32–66 *passim*. The accounts of Bulwer-Lytton *vis-à-vis* Elliotson and Home come from Robert Lee Wolff, *Strange Stories and Other Explorations in Victorian Fiction* (Boston: Gambit, 1971), pp. 237 and 246; that of Jennings, from Michael Howard, *The Occult Conspiracy* (London: Rider, 1989), p. 108.

Zadkiel's letter concerning 'Hartiel' was to his friend J. E. 'Shepherd' Smith, the editor of *The Family Herald*. It is quoted from W. A. Smith, *'Shepherd' Smith the Universalist* (London: Sampson Law, 1892), p. 412. See also Smith's *The Coming Man* (London: Strahan & Co., 1873), 2 vols, ch. XLII on astrology. (I am grateful to Elaine Jordan for bringing Smith to my attention.)

For an example of biblical interdiction of divination, see Deuteronomy xvii.12. The usual counter-example is that of the Magi.

NB: There is a contemporary 'review' of *Zadkiel's Almanac for 1849* by a leading critic of 'superstition', Augustus de Morgan, who was a professor of mathematics at University College London and a frequent contributor to the *Athenaeum*. It is reprinted in his *A Budget of Paradoxes* (London: Longmans, Greene & Co., 1872), pp. 277–84. In fact, de Morgan hardly deigns to mention his putative subject, slipping immediately into a meditation on coincidence mixed with personal anecdotes with the same smug arrogance that modern writers on the subject like Douglas Hofstadter, Martin Gardner, James Randi and Patrick Moore exhibit. The continuity is striking. See George P. Hansen, 'CSICOP and the Skeptics: An Overview', *The Journal of the American Society for Psychical Research* LXXXVI (1992), 19–63.

A. J. Pearce and Richard Garnett

I would like to thank Annabella Kitson for first urging me to consider Pearce. I have used his own writings as mentioned in my text; and, in addition, a brief biography in *Old Moore's Monthly Messenger* VII (June 1914), pp. 170–2 and the obituary of Pearce in *The Occult Review* XXXVII:5 (May 1923), pp. 339–44. I have also drawn on Pearce's unpublished papers, which his great-granddaughter Ms Tina Whitehead very kindly made available to me, in addition to helping with various questions I had. Pearce's correspondence with *The Lancet* appears in the issues for 13 December 1913 and 3 January 1914. Circulation figures for *Zadkiel's Almanac* occasionally appeared in *Zadkiel's Almanac* and on p. 149 of *The Science of the Stars*. The account of Pearce's meeting with Garnett in the British Museum appears in *Zadkiel's Almanac for 1907*, pp. 85–6; his quote regarding Theosophical astrology from *Star Lore* No. 8 (August 1897), p. 120; concerning magic, *Urania* No. 9 (September 1880); regarding his target constituency, *The Science of the Stars*, p. 149.

Pearce also published *The Science of the Stars* (London: Simpkin, 1881; reprinted by Glen, 1898); *The Weather Guide-Book* (London: Simpkin, Marshall, 1864); and three other journals in addition to his regular almanac: *Urania* (1880), *The Future* (1892–4) and *Star Lore and Future Events* (1897–1903).

The quotation by Stewart and Lockyer (which I would like to thank Simon Schaffer for bringing to my attention) is taken from p. 323 of Greg Myers,

'Thermodynamics and Social Prophecy', pp. 307–38 in *Energy and Entropy: Science and Culture in Victorian Britain*, ed. Patrick Brantlinger (Bloomington IN: Indiana University Press, 1989). That of R. A. Proctor comes from A. J. Meadows, *Science and Controversy: A Biography of Sir Norman Lockyer* (London: Macmillan, 1972), p.98. Proctor wrote many books of popular astronomy. A typical example of his attacks on astrology in newspaper articles is 'The Humbug of Astrology', *The New York World* (6 February 1887). (L. D. Broughton was the astrologer who replied most fully.)

Richard Garnett's birth-data appears in A. J. Pearce's *Star Lore* III:24 (December 1899), p. 54, where the former's nativity was published with his consent; and in Wilde and Dodson (see immediately below), p. 183. Pearce also published Garnett's obituary in *Zadkiel's Almanac* (1907), pp. 85–6. I would like to thank Clive Kavan for making both of these available. Another astrological obituary appeared in Alan Leo's *Modern Astrology* XVII/III:6 (June 1906), pp. 269–73 and XVII/III:7 (July 1906), pp. 300–10. (George Wilde in his *Treatise* (see below), p. 183, gives a birth-time of 5.50 p.m. Like Pearce, Wilde knew Garnett. *The Forecast* I:2 (1906), p.38, edited by Sepharial, gives 5.30 p.m. — almost certainly wrong.)

'The Soul and the Stars', written under Garnett's pseudonym of A. G. Trent, first appeared in *The University Magazine* (March 1880), pp. 334–46. (It was available as a booklet from Leo's 'International Publishing Co.', 39 Imperial Buildings, Ludgate Circus, in 1893.) It was then reprinted, revised and extended, in G. Wilde and J. Dodson's *A Treatise of Natal Astrology* (Halifax: for the authors, 1894), pp. i–xxix.

In addition to Garnett's own writings, I have used the above-mentioned obituaries; Carolyn G. Heilbrun, *The Garnett Family* (London: George Allen and Unwin, 1961); the entry in the *DNB* (Supplement for 1901–11), pp. 79–82; *The Hampstead Annual* (1906–7); *The Biographical Press Agency: Dr Richard Garnett* (1903); and Richard Garnett, *Constance Garnett: A Heroic Life* (London: Sinclair-Stevenson, 1991), where the horoscope for David Garnett is reported on p. 77. Garnett's correspondence to *The Spectator* appears in the issue for 22 February 1862, pp. 209–10. To some extent, Heilbrun's book has been superseded by Barbara McCrimmon, *Richard Garnett: The Scholar as Librarian* (London: American Library Association, 1989), although I prefer the former — not least because McCrimmon devotes not a word to Garnett's astrology, however much it may have been a matter of interest to him. The omission is all the more exasperating given her thoroughness in other respects.

The episode of Garnett and Ralph Shirley comes from a letter by the latter which appeared in *The Morning Leader* of 15 April 1905; it was reprinted in the obituary in *Modern Astrology*, p. 271. Garnett's objection to the use of the word 'occult' is also mentioned in the obituary in *Modern Astrology*, p. 309. In addition, his astrological premonition, if such it was, of his death is quoted therein on p. 305. (His final address in Hampstead, incidentally, was 27 Tanza Road.)

Samuel Butler's correspondence comes from Henry Festing Jones, *Samuel Butler, Author of Erewhon (1835–1902). A Memoir*, vol. I (London: Macmillan, 1919), 2 vols, I, pp. 388–9. A. R. Wallace's quotations appear in *Zadkiel's Almanac for 1923*, p. 73 and A. J. Pearce's *Text-Book of Astrology* (2nd edn, 1911), p. 73.

On the Society for Psychical Research, see Janet Oppenheim, *The Other World: Spiritualism and Psychical Research in England, 1850–1914* (Cambridge: Cambridge University Press, 1985).

In addition to Tina Whitehead, I would also like to thank Lucas Siorvanes for his suggestions, and Richard Garnett for not only kindly providing me with his great-grandfather's photograph, but helpfully commenting on the second half of the chapter.

Alan Leo

I would like to thank Nicholas Campion for helpful information on the proliferation of contemporary astrological organizations; Jacques Halbronn for bibliographical information; Maggie Hyde for her lecture on 'Alan Leo's Dream', on 12 July 1990 and for letting me see part of her forthcoming book (see my concluding references, below) in advance; the Astrological Lodge of the Theosophical Society for lending me the original photograph of the Leos in France and Alan Leo's pen and seal to photograph; and especially Tim Lethbridge, who went out of his way to make available to me both the minutes of the 'Middlesex Lodge' and a trunk of Alan Leo's unpublished manuscripts, press cuttings and letters which was discovered only a few years ago.

The birth-data for Alan Leo comes from the journal which Leo and Lacey took over, *The Astrologer* (February 1890). (Note, however, *The Life and Work of Alan Leo*, p. 42, where Lacey states that Leo 'always understood that he was born at 6 a.m.'.) The former time gives an ascendant of 0° 50′ Virgo, which may be why he 'rectified' the time to 5.49 — as stated, for example, in Bessie Leo et al., *The Life and Work of Alan Leo, Theosophist-Astrologer-Mason* (London: L. N. Fowler, 1919), p. 175, which gives an ascendant of 27° 36′ Leo. (This was rather greedy, since he already had four planets in Leo anyway; or he may have believed that Leo is a better or more fortunate sign than Virgo — a debatable proposition, except perhaps for someone with their Sun in Leo.)

(The time of Leo and Lacey's decision on 21 November 1889 to start a new periodical is not given, but the map published in Bessie Leo, *Life and Work*, p. 30, shows 1° 23′ Capricorn ascending, and 7° 00′ Scorpio on the midheaven.)

Bessie Leo was born at 6.47.12 p.m. (obviously a rectified time) on 5 April

1858, in Salisbury. She died at 12.30 a.m. on 23 May 1931. (This information was taken from a notice of a memorial service.)

Biographical information for Alan and Bessie Leo comes from Bessie Leo et al.; Bessie Leo, *Astrological Essays* (London: L. N. Fowler, 1909); Alan Leo, *The Astrologer and His Work* (London: L. N. Fowler, 1911); 'Alan Leo', *Old Moore's Monthly Messenger* VII:3 (December 1913), pp. 50–2; the memorial issue of *Modern Astrology*, XXVIII/XIV:12 (December 1917); 'Alan Leo: An Appreciation', pp. 343–9 in *The Occult Review* XXVI (December 1917); and *The Co-Mason* IX (1917), pp. 139–40. (Thanks to Patricia Fara for bringing the last to my attention.) Leo's *Esoteric Astrology* contains an autobiography by Bessie Leo, pp. 207–26.

The court case concerning Bessie's father's will is described in *Modern Astrology* XX/VI:9 (September 1909), pp. 385–8. (With *Modern Astrology* I supply both old — that is, regarded as a continuation of *The Astrologer's Magazine* — and new volume numbers.) Test horoscopes are discussed in *Modern Astrology* XIV/I:6 (December 1903), pp. 183–91, and XXI:VII (June 1910), p. 222. The 1914 trial is discussed in *Modern Astrology* XXV/XI (July 1914), pp. 289–393, *The Times* of 7 May 1914; and the *Star* of 6 May 1914. The 1917 trial is discussed in *Modern Astrology* XXVIII/XIV (September 1917), pp. 257–87, 303–6; *The Times* of 10 and 17 July 1917; the *Star* of 9 July 1917; and the *Daily News* of 17 April 1917. Leo's death is described in *Modern Astrology* XXVIII:XIV:10 (October 1917). His dream is recounted in Bessie Leo et al., p. 141.

Leo's call to modernize astrology comes from the first issue of *Modern Astrology* (August 1895); his reference to inequalities from Bessie Leo et al., p. 11. The long quotation by Bessie Leo on Theosophical astrology comes from her *Astrological Essays*, pp. 1, 4–5, 162, 168. The opening quotation by E. H. Bailey comes from his magazine *Destiny* I:5 (May 1905), p. 135.

For information on the 'Middlesex Lodge' I have used copies of its original minutes (in Bessie Leo's hand); the lecture by Mrs Rhodes delivered to the Astrological Lodge on 13 January 1930; Charles E. O. Carter, 'The Astrological Lodge of the Theosophical Society', *In Search* II: 1 (1959), 9–14; Geoffrey Cornelius, 'The Astrological Lodge from Alan Leo to the Present Day', *Astrology* LX:1 (1986), pp. 30–43; and Ronald C. Davison, 'The Astrological Lodge', *Astrology* LX:2 (1987) pp. 90–3.

Sources used for R. H. Penny and his case ('Penny vs. Hanson', 18QBD478) were his letter in *Modern Astrology* (September 1899) pp. 73–4; *Knowledge* (1888) (this was a journal edited by Richard A. Proctor); *The Occult Review* XIX:6 (1914), p. 300; and the *British Journal of Astrology* XII (August 1919) p. 121. Penny died on 25 February 1919.

Biographical information for Sepharial/W. G. Old (including his birth-data) comes principally from his biography by C. Sherburn in *Old Moore's Monthly*

Messenger VII:2 (November 1913) pp. 30–3. The quotations by Old on astrology are from, respectively, his *New Manual of Astrology* (London: W. Foulsham, 1898), p. x; *Prognostic Astronomy* (London: L. N. Fowler, 1901), p.7; and *Old Moore's Monthly Messenger* (November 1913). Sepharial quotes Lodge in p. vi of the *New Manual*. I also gained some insight into Sepharial from my discussions with Roger Parisious.

E. H. Bailey's lecture comes from the *British Journal of Astrology* XII (May 1919), p. 107. Bailey states in the *Journal* XXIII (September 1930), p. 243 that he was born 'in the morning' (he estimates 7.45 a.m.) on 29 November 1876; he gives no place. In *Old Moore's Monthly Messenger* (which he also edited) VII (March 1914), however, it states on pp. 90–2 that Bailey was born at 0.55 p.m.; and that the place was 1°E 18'/51°N 15' in East Kent. (The same volume, the number for April 1914, pp. 130–2 also supplies George Wilde's birth-data: 11.30 p.m., 16 April 1860, Leeds.)

For further reading on the Theosophical milieu, see Janet Oppenheim's useful *The Other World: Spiritualism and Psychical Research in England, 1850–1914* (Cambridge: Cambridge University Press, 1985). In addition to Oppenheim, I have used Michael Gomes, *The Dawning of the Theosophical Movement* (Wheaton, IL: Theosophical Publishing, 1987); and Mary Lutyens, *Krishna-murti: The Years of Awakening* (NY: Avon, 1975). I am also grateful to Joy Dixon for our discussions; see her forthcoming Ph.D. on Theosophy and women, from Rutgers University.

NB: Leo's *Esoteric Astrology* was neither the last nor the worst on the subject. Compared to Alice Bailey's book of the same name, first published in 1951, for example, it remains a model of clarity and precision. However, it was surpassed in both respects by C. E. O. Carter's essay 'The Zodiac and the Soul' (London: Theosophical Publishing House, 1968), a work which Richard Garnett probably would have appreciated.

Conclusion

In addition to those whom I thanked in my Acknowledgements, all of whom contributed something to this chapter, I would like to thank John Elsom for a very helpful discussion.

For some interesting comments on 'the shift of emphasis from "character", which is the unity of moral codes and disciplined purpose, to an emphasis on "personality", which is the enhancement of self through the compulsive search for individual differentiation' — of which Leo's work is to some extent symptomatic — see Daniel Bell, *The Cultural Contradictions of Capitalism* (London: Heinemann, 1979, 2nd edn) — quoted here from p. xxiv.

The quotation by Michael Longley comes from an interview in the *Irish*

Times, 11 January 1992; that of Josef Skvorecky, later in the chapter, comes from a BBC TV interview broadcast in 1991.

Since Dane Rudhyar, one of the most influential 'Jungian' astrologers has been Liz Greeene, e.g. in *Saturn. A New Look at an Old Devil* (New York: Samuel Weiser, 1976).

For Mercury as the planetary ruler of astrologers and diviners, see William Lilly, *Christian Astrology* (London: Regulus, 1985; originally published 1647), p. 78.

Alan Leo on horary astrology comes from *Modern Astrology* II/VII:10 (1896), pp. 434–7; cf. (to the same effect) the Preface in his *Practical Astrology* (London: Modern Astrology, 1898, 2nd edn). A. J. Pearce on the same subject comes from his *Science of the Stars* (London: Simpkin, 1898, 2nd edn), p. 149. Note that he dropped horary entirely from the second edition (1911) of his *Text-Book of Astrology* (London: for the author, 1879, 1889). It is worth recalling his remark in the latter, volume II, p. 357: 'It is evident that there are many perplexities in horary astrology; and that those mystics and occultists who so greatly affect it have much work before them if those problems are capable of solution.'

The recent revival of interest in horary astrology is partly the cause, partly the result of two recent books: Derek Appleby, *Horary Astrology: An Introduction to the Art of Time* (Wellingborough: Aquarian Press, 1985) and Olivia Barclay, *Horary Astrology Rediscovered* (West Chester PA: Whitford Press, 1990). Readers should also refer to the important work of Geoffrey Cornelius, whose book should appear in 1993, and Maggie Hyde, whose *Jung and Astrology* will be published by Aquarian Press in 1992.

The passage by James Smith comes from p. 360–1 of his *The Coming Man* (London: Strahan and Co., 1873), 2 vols, chapter XLII: 'Astrology: Its General Truth Maintained and Defended, in Spite of its Particular Failures and Professional Quackery'. (Smith was writing in 1848). I am grateful to Elaine Jordan for telling me about him.

The quotation by Carlyle comes from John Stuart Mill, *On Liberty* (London: Penguin, 1974), pp. 81–2 where he slightly misquotes Carlyle by substituting 'but' for 'and'. The quotation by William Stukeley (1687–1765) comes from the Wellcome Institute MS. 54729.

For an excellent discussion of science, including its rationalism and universalism, in relation to my own herein, see Paul Feyerabend, *Farewell to Reason* (London: Verso, 1987). The historical connections of science and magic have been the subject of considerable scholarly debate, much of it generated by Frances Yates, *Giordano Bruno and the Hermetic Tradition* (London: Routledge and Kegan Paul, 1964). For more recent work on the subject, see Charles Webster, *From Paracelsus to Newton: Magic and the Making of Modern Science* (Cambridge: Cambridge University Press, 1982). Note also the work of G. E. R. Lloyd, *Magic, Reason and Experience: Studies in the Origins and Development of Greek Science* (Cambridge University Press, 1979).

James Stuart Mill's works, particularly his *On Liberty* (1859) and *Autobiography* (1873) are still widely available. For a modern commentary and extension thereof, see Isaiah Berlin, *Four Essays on Liberty* (Oxford: Oxford University Press, 1969); I have quoted here from p. 192. For a related analysis from a different perspective, see Ernesto Laclau, *New Reflections on the Revolution of Our Time* (London: Verso, 1990); Richard Rorty, *Contingency, Irony and Solidarity* (Cambridge: Cambridge University Press, 1989); and Feyerabend. These three authors I take to be significantly extending and developing Mill's programme, although it still awaits proper 'greening'. (NB: By 'life-affirming' I certainly do not mean just human life. The universal right to life as a maxim is itself, of course, open to abuse. That is unavoidable, albeit certainly contestable.)

For a brief discussion that places alternative and complementary epistemologies on the side of progressive social and political projects — at least potentially — see Paul Ekins, *A New World Order: Grassroots Movements for Global Change* (London: Routledge, 1992), pp. 202–4 and also Feyerabend. For a counter-view, which I find ultimately unconvincing, see Rosalind Coward, *The Whole Truth: The Myth of Alternative Health* (London: Faber, 1989).

On an 'intelligent' universe, see Gregory Bateson, *Mind and Nature: A Necessary Unity* (New York: E. P. Dutton, 1979). On 'qualities', see also Owen Barfield, *The Rediscovery of Meaning, and Other Essays* (Middletown CN: Wesleyan University Press, 1977). For a fictional treatment of mythopoeic or symbolic thinking (along the lines of my list of astrological 'lessons') set in contemporary London, see Russell Hoban, *The Medusa Frequency* (London: Jonathan Cape, 1987). See also Brian Friel, *Faith Healer* (Loughcrew: The Gallery Press, 1991.)

INDEX